EXPECT TO WIN –

HATE TO LOSE

MATT FUREY

A Matt Furey Book

All rights reserved.

Copyright © 2011 by **Associated Creators, LP**

ISBN: 978-0-981-9320-4-0

Associated Creators, LP
10339 Birdwatch Dr.,
Tampa, Florida 33647, USA

Praise for
Expect To Win – Hate To Lose

"This book has the strength of a Siberian tiger, and yet all its inspiring physical lessons contain even deeper lessons for the mind and spirit. This is Matt's masterpiece—the most inspiring book I've ever read. I'm ready to take the mountain and keep climbing, and I will never stop reading this book."

*– **Steve Chandler***
*Author of **Time Warrior***

---

*"I think I've read over 1000 books on self-improvement, success, winning. None of them and I mean NONE OF THEM were as powerful as **Expect To Win – Hate To Lose**. If you are doing okay this book will make you a winner. If you're a winner this book will make you a champion. If you're a champion this book will put you in the Hall Of Fame. When I got my copy I sat down to read 20 or so pages... I read the whole thing. You will not be able to put it down. The book vibrates. **Expect To Win – Hate To Lose** is Matt at his best!"*

*– **Paul Reddick***
The Master of MPH

"Most of my life I expected to lose even though I wanted to win. I knew I had to expect to win, as every self-help expert would tell you. But none of them tells you HOW to expect to win, so I was at a loss. It had always been an empty slogan to me because I never knew the HOW. That was until 1999 when I became Matt Furey's student.

*He was the first one to tell me the actual process of winning and how to expect it in everything I did. Only then did my life do a complete 180 and winning became easy. In Matt's **Expect to Win – Hate to Lose** he's put these actual steps on paper in an entertaining, simple and inspirational way. There's no fluff, no nonsense, no confusion – just real meat that cuts right to the bone. Any person who wants to win in every aspect of life needs this book. It's the fastest, easiest way to win."*

*– **Ed Baran***
*Author of **Gymnastic Abs***

---

*"**Expect to Win – Hate to Lose** by Matt Furey provides you with a potent cocktail for unlimited success, which anyone serious should be lining up to drink. As a modern day philosopher, Matt Furey is a man you want to be learning from and listening to. No exceptions. No excuses!"*

– Trevor 'ToeCracker' Crook
www.TrevorCrookBlog.com

---

*"**Expect to Win – Hate to Lose** MUST be in the personal library of every person who is striving to improve. From the moment you open the book, Matt Furey becomes your own personal guide to success. So think of this book as a treasure map leading you to your pot of gold. Chapter after chapter is jam-packed with priceless knowledge. I found my "pot of gold" in chapters 55 and 56, which revealed everything I didn't realize about my success mechanism. After reading this material, I found myself moving through the quagmire of procrastination like a hot knife through butter... getting more accomplished in the last few weeks than I have all year. And, without any radical changes. That kind of guidance is priceless!"*

– Steve Grzymkowski
www.thefamilyaffect.com

"Wow! I couldn't stop reading this book. Matt relays so much positive information that can immediately be put to action. His stories are seriously inspiring! He makes so much sense and gives amazing, yet simple, techniques for physical and mental self-improvement. I will recommend this book to every coach, athlete, trainer, client, parent or future parent I come across."

– Uncle Mike Stehle, ATC
Co-owner, The Training Room

---

*"Looking for a book that will jump-start you both personally and professionally? Look no further. **Matt Furey's Expect To Win – Hate To Lose** is the wake up call that will help you reach your true potential. Clear and concise, this book can be the catylist to getting everything you want out of life if you heed Matt's expert advice."*

– Pat Rigsby
Co-Owner, Athletic Revolution International

*"In **Expect to Win – Hate to Lose**, Matt Furey swings the bat and rips the cover right off the ball!*

As I read each precious chapter, I began to experience feelings of exuberance, enlightenment, inspiration and prosperity. I became extremely excited about the various opportunities I wish to create in my own future, while finally unraveling some of the unsolved mysteries of my past. The more I read, the more my imagination ran wild with endless possibility and confidence. Yet, at other times, I found myself humbled by Matt's extraordinary wisdom and remarkable insights into so many crucial areas of life.

Indeed, a book this powerful could have only been written by the hand of a true Master. Read it... bask in its vast knowledge, as did I... and you too will be given the keys to the kingdom of unlimited success."

*– **Rob Colasanti***
Ambassador of the Martial Arts

To the winner within you!

Introduction

Several years ago I began writing a monthly column for Inside Kung-Fu magazine that became an instant hit with martial artists around the globe. At the same time, similar writings about success in emails at MattFurey.com and Psycho-Cyb.com caused a positive roar from friends, fans and customers. For years many people have suggested I compile a book from my columns and emails – and after thinking about it, I decided to release **Expect To Win – Hate To Lose**.

At first, I planned to publish all my martial arts columns exactly as I wrote them. But when I looked at the appeal my emails have had with athletes from virtually any sport, as well as success-minded people who want to know the inner secrets that produce championship results, I decided to edit the columns and make them less martial artsy and more inclusive of the world outside of Inside Kung Fu.

What Kung Fu Means

When you consider the true meaning for the words "kung fu" – pronounced **gong fu** in Chinese, you may agree with my decision. Why? Because in Chinese, the term **gong fu** doesn't mean the study of martial arts. It means "skill acquired through dedicated practice."

If you're a master chef, you have great cooking *gong fu*.

If you're a virtuoso on the violin, you have tremendous musical *gong fu*.

If you're a champion debater, you have superb oratorical *gong fu*.

And if you read this entire book in one setting, from start to finish, you have great concentration *gong fu* and perhaps I have great writing *gong fu*, or we have a combination of the two.

My deepest wish is that the principles, concepts, secrets and strategies in **Expect to Win – Hate to Lose** move you to get the most out of yourself, and out of life itself. May all your goals come to fruition beyond what you can currently imagine.

—*Matt Furey*
May 2011

Contents

Chapter 1: Expect to Win 1

Chapter 2: Talent is Useless 4

Chapter 3: Aaron Rodgers' Secret 7

Chapter 4: Coaches Who Don't Talk About It 11

Chapter 5: The Power of Positive Practice 14

Chapter 6: Silence is Golden 17

Chapter 7: The Power of One Move 21

Chapter 8: Knock Down This Wall 24

Chapter 9: Suffer Now, Live it Up Later. 27

Chapter 10: Excellence or Fun? 30

Chapter 11: What You Picture in Your Mind Matters 35

Chapter 12: 2 Kinds of Pride. 38

Chapter 13: Tough Times Never Last 41

Chapter 14: The Biggest Competitor You Will Ever Face. 44

Chapter 15: Competence vs. Confidence. 48

Chapter 16: Breathe More – Do More. 53

Chapter 17: The Legs Feed the Wolf. 57

Chapter 18: 90 Days of Non-stop Walking 60

Chapter 19: It's A Secret to You 64

Chapter 20: Backward Training. 68

Chapter 21: Upside Down Training 72

Chapter 22: Be True to Yourself 75

Chapter 23: The Power of a Focused Mind 78

Chapter 24: Be Willing to Move Heaven and Earth 82

Chapter 25: Believing is Seeing 85

Chapter 26: Burn the Past 88

Chapter 27: Counting Leads to Success. 91

Chapter 28: Do The Thing You Fear 94

Chapter 29: Don't Make It Harder Than It Is 97

Chapter 30: Get Out of Town 100

Chapter 31: Gold Medal Clues 104

Chapter 32: How to Get Good Faster. 106

Chapter 33: How Strong is Your Desire? 109

Chapter 34: How to Stop Losing and Start Winning. 113

Chapter 35: I Dare You to Succeed 115

Chapter 36: The Secret Power of 'S' 118

Chapter 37: Your Hidden Strength 122

Chapter 38: Keep Climbing. 125

Chapter 39: Laser Focus 128

Chapter 40: Laugh in the Face of Pain 131

Chapter 41: The Element of Surprise 134

Chapter 42: Smile in the Face of Fear. 137

Chapter 43: Listen, Believe, Apply 141

Chapter 44: On Fathers and Father Figures 144

Chapter 45: Good to Great. 148

Chapter 46: Picture Your Previous Victories 151

Chapter 47: Power in the Joints 154

Chapter 48: Pushup Poker 158

Chapter 49: Remember to Remember 161

Chapter 50: Breathe Like a Samurai. 165

Chapter 51: Connect the Mind to the Body 168

Chapter 52: Slaying Demons 171

Chapter 53: So You Want to be a Master? 174

Chapter 54: Vengeance or Virtue? 177

Chapter 55: Give Yourself a Clean Slate 180

Chapter 56: Where Everything Starts 183

Chapter 57: Your Imaginary Training Partner 186

Chapter 58: Find Your Success Groove 190

Chapter 59: The Powder of Champions 193

Chapter 60: 1% More 196

Chapter 61: Your Great Leap Forward 200

Chapter 62: Hate to Lose 204

The author training before a banyan tree in Bermuda.

1

Expect to Win

"My mind is my biggest asset. I expect to win every tournament I play."

– Tiger Woods

In December of 1997, my teammates and I met for practice in Cupertino, California, to get ready for the World Shuaijiao Kung fu Championships, to be held over Christmas in Beijing, China. Before practice began, each member of the team was asked to give a quote that would go into a Team U.S.A. program we would give as gifts to other teams.

Without delay I said: "I never go into a competition expecting to lose. I go into it expecting to win – and win I do."

It was cocky of me to say this. It was even cockier to have this statement go into the programs we were giving out. Yet, because it was how I truly felt in my heart, I let the quote stand. And I am glad I did.

Prove What You Mean

Expecting to win is not the same as wanting to win. It's not the same as having a strong, burning desire to succeed. It's higher up the scale.

When your desire to win turns into an expectation, your vibration is so strong you go into a calm, relaxed-ready state. You've put in your training time. You've mentally rehearsed what you intend to do in your imagination so many times you can taste victory. Now you've got to prove that actions speak louder than words; that what you've imagined will become a reality.

The bottom line is that you have no right to expect success if you do nothing to bring it about. You need to practice. A LOT. You imagine what you want, you see yourself excited about achieving what you want, then you make a vow to do WHATEVER it takes to make it happen. This is true in sports, in fitness, in business and in everything else.

You don't make excuses. You make progress. You set your mind on a target, you get a mental picture of it, then you MOVE. The big mistake is to simply sit and ponder, then wonder why nothing is happening.

Sure, sometimes you get lucky. Sometimes you can sit on the sideline and miraculously good things will happen. But that's not how fighting works, nor competition of any kind. The person who refuses to get off his chair and enter the arena is not going to succeed.

Whatever It Takes

Whenever someone says he has goals but is not seeing them realized, look at whether he is willing to do whatever it takes to win. I'm betting he's not. He'll do a little bit and if results don't come immediately, he'll get frustrated. Or impatient. He'll put time limits on the process. He'll say he "should already be" where he wants to be.

Wrong moves.

As I tell my students, "Fear, frustration and impatience are not part of the success process." Get over them. Challenge your mind to be free of the negative clutter that keeps your life in neutral. Do what champions do: When success eludes them, they focus more—not less. They recommit. They get tough.

Many people think of today's world as being filled with crybabies who are trying to whine their way to the top. Well, here's how I view the concept of being babied.

Observe the baby. He falls down 1,000 times and gets up 1,000 times. Even so, no matter what, you never hear a parent say to their baby, "Oh Johnny, you've fallen so many times. You poor baby. You've worked so hard. I think you should try something else. How about crawling? Maybe that's better for you."

Treat Ourselves Better

It's hard to imagine a parent treating his child this way. It would be cruel, don't you think? Yet, this is what we often do to ourselves when faced with a challenge. We get an idea to claim our dream, to stake out our goal. Then we get whacked. We make mistakes and fail. And we think these are signs that we "can't." Not true.

Some people give up the first time they get whacked. Others give up after 100 whacks. But the champions, the masters, the really great ones, can get whacked 1,000 times and they still won't quit. They'll keep on until they claim their prize. Instead of seeing mistakes as something to avoid, they view their mistakes as corrective feedback leading them to their goal.

The same mindset applies to any endeavor you want to be successful. The more you fail, the more you fall down, the closer you are to success. Be not discouraged if you make a mistake. Fear not your failures and setbacks. If there is anything to fear, it is giving up when you are inches from success, but don't know it.

Train to win. Pour your mind into practice time. Go to bed thinking about what you want to accomplish and wake up with your vision playing inside your head. Cultivate a spirit of relaxed readiness that tells the world you don't just want to win – you expect to win – and win you will.

2

Talent is Useless

"Talent is useless without training, thank God."

– Mark Twain

One of the greatest curses of humankind is being someone who possesses enormous natural talent along with a lack of desire to use it. Many people think that talent alone is all you need; or they assume talent and desire go hand-in-hand. They often don't.

True, talent and genetics play a role in everything we do in life, but far too many people swallow genetic fact with genetic theory. It's a fact that our height, eye color, hair color and skin color are genetic. Even our propensity to be good at certain skills can be genetic.

But whether or not we choose to develop our talents is not genetic. It's environmental. Many potential "great ones" never make it, regardless of their predisposition to being successful because they lacked the successful structure that brings the greatness out.

Your Success Environment

Give a person a success environment and you can work miracles. You can take the average and ordinary and help them become extraordinary. You can take the "non-gifted" and make others think they're naturals. You can even take the sick, lowly and disabled and make them powerful.

When I mention 'environment' I am not just speaking of the space outside of you. I am also talking about what goes into your mind. Why? Because regardless of a person's environment or talent, if you set up a success environment in your own mind, you can overcome seemingly insurmountable obstacles.

For example, an athlete who's missing two arms and two legs does not have a genetic advantage. He doesn't have more skills or more innate ability. Yet, what **Dustin Carter** does have is an environment that fosters success. And because of this, along with his willingness to practice, he wins again and again. Go to **youtube.com** and type in the following to see what I mean: **"No Arms, No Legs, All Heart-Dustin Carter Documentary Teaser."**

Watch this video then ask yourself if you really want to succumb to the philosophy that equates success with nothing more than genetics. Yes, there are genetic advantages, but without the willingness to practice, practice, practice, they usually don't amount to much. Hence, the veracity of the Mark Twain quote, "Talent is useless without training, thank God." He could just as easily have substituted the word "genetics" for "talent" and the same would be true.

At the highest levels of sports, martial arts, music, art and industry, you'll find the people at the top didn't just land there because of talent. In most cases, both talent and the willingness to work, play an equal part.

It Takes More Than Big Feet to Win

Back in 2008 when Michael Phelps won eight gold medals in the Beijing Olympics, the media was quick to point out the genetic advantages Phelps had. First of all, he was tall. Second, he had huge flipper-like feet with very flexible ankles.

Although these physical attributes are true, it didn't replace the fact that if Phelps didn't train as hard as he did, he wouldn't have won a single gold medal, much less eight. Without a great coach as well as his own willingness to push himself to the brink, he would have easily lost to those who don't have flipper-like feet.

Far too often, those with the most talent are NOT willing to do the training that will develop their talent to the full. Those who make it are the ones who are hungry, ready and willing to compensate for lack of talent with something called relentless repetition.

Rising to the top through relentless repetition and dedicated enthusiastic practice is only part of the journey, though. Remaining at the top of your game also requires practice because the easiest thing to forget is what got you where you are.

One Hundred Times a Day

For an athlete, practicing a specific technique a hundred times a day, or even a thousand times a day, may lead him to the top. But it would be a major mistake to think that once he's at the top he doesn't need to practice his skills anymore.

Let me put it to you this way, resting on your laurels leads to rusting on your skills. I've had to eat these words more than once. The easiest thing in the world is to get complacent or become casual about what it takes to get good and stay good. One of the beautiful things about sports is that we get to witness excellence on the way up as well as what the great ones must do to stay at the top.

Talent is useless, unless you're willing to develop it.

3

Aaron Rodgers' Secret

*"See things as you would have them be
instead of as they are."*

– Robert Collier

"The Zen of Football." That was the headline in a recent issue of **USA Today**. And on the front page of the Sports Section, I read: "Rodgers: Foreseeing is Believing."

In the article, Green Bay Packers Quarterback, Aaron Rodgers, talks about the power of visualization. He credits his daily mental practice in helping the Packers reach the post season, and for pounding the Atlanta Falcons, the #1 seed, 48-21.

This amazing victory was followed by another over NFC Division rival Chicago. And then it was off to the Super Bowl to face the Pittsburgh Steelers.

What people have quickly forgotten is this: Rodgers spent three seasons on the bench watching former teammate, Brett Favre, lead the Packers. He worked his tail off in the early years, with no visible results to show for it on the field. But this year, his third as a starter, he made believers out of his team as well as everyone else.

Rodgers says he learned how to visualize from a coach, when he was in 6th grade. He also says most of the big plays he made in Green Bay's upset victory over Atlanta, were pictured in his imagination first.

It's amazing to me that this story is headline news in today's world. You would think with all the information available on the power of your creative imagination this would be considered such a "ho hum, of course" story that no one would care. After all, how many great athletes don't visualize in one form or another? Some use self-hypnosis. Some visualize while lying down. Some while sitting. I even teach people to do it while standing still or moving.

No matter how you visualize though, the key thing to remember is that it won't work unless your practice creates what Dr. Maxwell Maltz, author of **Psycho-Cybernetics**, calls "that winning feeling."

You've Got to Feel It

Many people visualize but don't feel anything. This is a red flag that something they are doing is wrong. Visualization without a change of emotion isn't the proper use of your creative imagination.

That's one of the reasons I believe a more powerful approach to mind training is to change your feelings before you visualize. This can be accomplished through deep breathing, stillness or through movements that integrate the breath.

E-motion stands for energy with movement. It's great to sit or lie still and picture what you want. But it's much more effective to train your mind like a fighter who is shadow boxing an imaginary foe.

Shadow boxing is a term used to describe a practice used by top boxers, martial artists, wrestlers, salespeople, speakers, golfers as well as surgeons. You don't just picture yourself doing the thing. You go through the motions as you picture it and you make sure you FEEL it.

Out of a Slump

Last Spring a big-time slugger in Major League Baseball was in a terrible slump. He'd forgotten what he'd done in previous years to hit the ball out of the park with power and confidence. He was doubting himself like never before. The last time I worked with him, I had him

The author works on shoulder of MLB slugger Carlos Pena.

shadow batting, hitting homeruns in an imaginary setting we concocted at his beach front condo.

After 15 minutes of active imagination, he said to me, "This is great. I feel like a kid again. This is how it was in the beginning when everything was new to me and I was so grateful just to be on a team in the Major Leagues."

The slugger wanted to know how quickly the shadow batting would work for him. I was reluctant to give him a time frame, but finally said to him: "If you practice this once a day, within a week I think you'll be slamming homeruns again."

One week later, while on vacation in China, it was a daily thrill for me to read about his homerun spree. In six games, he knocked seven out of the park.

Setting up a success environment isn't difficult. All you need is a chair to sit still on or a small place to "shadow box" whatever you want to accomplish. Then make sure you choose the most powerful and emotionalized thoughts to play on the screen of your mind.

At the same time, make sure you strike from your mind any thought that talent alone will get you to the top, as well as the mistaken notion that someone else will remain better than you because he or she has more talent or is already ahead of you. It's not where you start that's important – it's where you finish. Someone may be ahead of you now, but if you're willing to suspend the idea of talent and genetics being everything, and you're willing to concentrate on being the best you can be, you'll be amazed at how far and how fast you'll travel.

When all is said and done, like Aaron Rodgers, you'll be able to tell someone how you pictured and played it all out ahead of time in your mind's eye. What you say will probably be a secret to the person who hears it, but it may lead to another champion in the making.

4

Coaches Who
Don't Talk About It

"Whoever said, 'It's not whether you win or lose that counts,' probably lost."

– Martina Navratilova

In my forty years of involvement in sports and martial arts, I've seen good coaches, incredible coaches and some really bad coaches. I've been trained by Olympic and world champions, by national champions and by masters and grand masters.

The very best coaches never emphasized winning as the only thing. At the same time, they were sure disappointed when I lost, and they let me know, with words, gestures and facial expressions, that they expected more from me in the future.

Some coaches handled failure poorly. I did at times, as well. But once I went back into the training hall to practice, the pain of defeat could be turned into something positive.

Demonstrate Success

Great coaches don't tell you what it takes to get to the top. They demonstrate it. They teach you how to handle failure. It's called keeping your head up and getting back to work as soon as possible, sometimes immediately after a contest.

Great coaches also teach you how to handle victory, which means no resting on one's laurels.

Without a doubt, there have been moments when a coach said the wrong thing to me. Occasionally, I got called a name I didn't like. But of all the words said to me that I didn't like, two de-motivators stand out.

Don't Pop Off Too Soon

The first was when a coach called me "champ" before a tournament began. In almost every case, whenever I was called "champ" before a competition began, I lost.

In baseball, withholding praise until the end of a game is commonplace, and a good practice others could learn. Far too many business deals are lost because the person getting the deal "pops off" and tells others before the check is in his hands and the papers are signed.

The second de-motivator happened before I ran out on the mat to compete. The coach shook my hand, looked me in the eyes and said, "Go out there and have fun." I did anything but have fun in that match. And today, every time I hear coaches in youth sports talking about "having fun," I remember that match.

I agree with having fun in sports, in business and in life. At the same time I think it's important to explain to an athlete what fun is and what it isn't. In my early 20's, when a coach told me to go out there and have fun, my mind drew a blank. I didn't have the foggiest idea what he was talking about.

What is Fun?

If you'd ask me today, I'd say that fun is going out and giving it everything you've got to win the game. Fun is executing the techniques you've practiced flawlessly. Fun is breaking records. Fun is giving more than you think you've got. Fun is playing with enthusiasm, it's hustling on every play and being courageous in the midst of fear, worry or self-doubt.

If the same coach who told me to go out and have fun had said, "Stay loose and relax, give it everything you've got and mop the floor with this guy" – I would have been motivated, rather than de-motivated.

So I'm concerned when I hear coaches telling athletes to "have fun" with no explanation of what fun looks like. To a 10-year old, having fun could very well mean playing with his X-Box, watching tee-vee or running around in ADD mode. So fun needs to be explained.

While working with my son's youth baseball team I explained to the boys what fun is. Fun is practicing what you love. Fun is playing the game you love with a good attitude. Fun is realizing you'll make mistakes and learn how to correct them.

The late John Wooden, never talked to his athletes at UCLA about winning, and he coached his team to 10 NCAA titles in 12 years. On the other hand, Wooden never talked to his athletes about having fun. In fact, he created a **Pyramid of Success**, with the building blocks of what it takes to succeed. And the two cornerstones on that Pyramid were industriousness (hard work) and enthusiasm. Wooden said he never saw anyone succeed in anything who didn't understand and employ those two principles.

Like Wooden, Dan Gable (who won 15 NCAA team titles in 21 seasons as head coach of the University of Iowa wrestling team), never really talked to us about winning. But he didn't need to because everyone on the Iowa wrestling team knew why he was on the team. To become a champion, individually, and as a team.

Our coach wanted us to win. He expected us to win because no team in the country trained as hard, or as often. Gable set the tone by doing far more than telling us to win. He demonstrated how to train in each and every practice. He was on the mat with us, sweating through everything we did.

If you ever have the privilege to be coached by someone who demonstrates success, you'll do everything you can to win for him.

5

The Power of
Positive Practice

*"I fear not the man who has practiced 10,000 kicks
once, but I fear the man who has practiced one kick
10,000 times."*

– Bruce Lee

In Chinese kung fu, if you'll do 1,000 repetitions per day of a single movement or skill, you'll own it. And if you'll commit to 1,000 reps a day for several years you will be a virtually unstoppable force.

Truth is the average person won't commit to 100 reps a day of anything, much less 10. And so, if you're the person who'll do 1,000 reps per day, you'll be so smooth and quick that even if someone knows what you're going to do, he still won't be able to stop you.

When I had my school in California it was common for me to teach a move that I had worked on for 10-20 years. It was also common for the non-champion student to go off and practice the move two or three times, then turn to me and say, "What's next, boss?"

"What's next? WHAT'S NEXT??? ARE YOU KIDDING ME? GET BACK TO WORK."

From Zero to Champion

Mitch was 0-13 in tournament karate competition when he began at age 12. His coach took him aside and told him the secret to winning. "Practice everyday – more than anyone else."

A month later, Bill "Superfoot" Wallace told him, "1,000 kicks per day, per leg."

Mitch followed what these champions told him. And within three months he wasn't just winning, he was destroying everyone he fought. His matches weren't even close. Mitch knew the secret of his success wasn't positive thinking, it was positive *practice*.

The Praying Mantis

Last year I met a lady in Manhattan who is a 7th generation praying mantis practitioner. Her father began teaching her at age seven, and for three years she was taught only one move. She practiced this move at least 1,000 times each day. After three years the foundation of her practice was far deeper than a single move, even though that is all she practiced. She was ready to learn much more and to absorb it quickly. Today, more than 30 years later, she is lightning fast, incredibly nimble and able to make you expend all your effort while she is barely breathing.

When working with my son, I have him execute the same throw over and over each day. I didn't teach him this throw exclusively for three years, but for far longer than anyone else I know. And when it came time for him to learn the next throw, it was amazing how quickly he got it. If, on the other hand, I taught him several throws on the same day, he probably wouldn't learn any of them very well. As Karl Gotch once told me, "If you don't want to teach them anything, show them everything."

50 Pitches Per Night

Pete Lillo told me the story of how he was able to throw a no-hitter: "My Dad had me throw 50 pitches a night through a tire hanging from a tree in our back yard. And I didn't get my evening meal until all 50 pitches went through the tire. By the time I was 16, I could put the ball in the strike zone anywhere I wanted."

If you think in terms of hours, one hour of practice per day will get you to 10,000 hours in 27.39 years. 30 minutes a day will take you 54.79 years.

But if you spend two hours per day, you'll get there in 13.69 years. Three hours per day will get you there in 9.13 years. Four hours per day will only take you 6.84 years. And if you put in eight hours per day you can reach mastery in 3.42 years.

Putting in an hour a day may seem impossible to you, especially over 27+ years. That's when a gentle reminder about concentrating on the number of repetitions per day makes the whole ball game much easier to play.

1,000 reps per day may not be practical for you. Perhaps 50-100 per day works better for you. You'll have to figure it out for whatever sport or art you practice. But one thing is for sure, the more reps you get, the better you will be.

Put the power of positive practice to work and you'll cause yourself to be successful in anything you do.

6

Silence is Golden

"Telling others your goals and plans often results in applause, followed by your unwillingness to follow through. You're better off zipping your lips until you've achieved your goal."

– Matt Furey

Many people have the idea that announcing your intentions is a good idea because the announcement, in and of itself, will force you to take action, and if you don't accomplish your goal, you'll suffer embarrassment and humiliation.

Fiddleschticks.

Since 1933 this idea has been tested and the results are always the same. If you talk about your goals before they happen, they're less likely to materialize.

Peter Gollwitzer, professor of psychology at NYU, recently published the results of new tests about whether to announce your intentions or keep your lips zipped (When Intentions Go Public: Does Social Reality Widen the Intention-Behavior Gap?"

Guess what Professor Gollwitzer found?

In four different tests of 63 people, those who kept their goals, intentions and plans to themselves were more likely to accomplish them than those who talked about them openly. Why? Because when you talk about your intentions, oftentimes you receive applause from others, and this applause replaces your willingness to do whatever it takes to make your goal become a reality. And if you don't receive applause, the negativity of others can also derail you.

It's a Bad Idea

Announcing your goals to the world is oftentimes a BAD idea for most people (I'll explain who it isn't a bad idea for in a few seconds). Before I tell you why this is so, keep in mind that I did NOT say you hide your goals from your master, mentor, advisor or coach.

How can a coach best help you if you won't tell him your goals? So it's good to let him know. But the world at large? No way.

Here are the reasons:

1. If you have ever had confidence problems or fear issues, and most people have, when you announce your goal to the "wrong people" – a good many of them may scoff, make fun or send negative vibes. Unless you already have the confidence of Muhammad Ali or Babe Ruth, this "talking before doing" can definitely derail you.

    In the early stages of goal achievement, when you're just starting to build confidence, you don't want to get unsolicited as well as unhelpful feedback from those who can't truly help you reach your destination. Let your master or mentor advise you and no one else.

2. In the movie, **Grand Canyon**, Steve Martin played a movie director. A man asked, "How's the new movie coming along." His reply – paraphrased: "I don't like to talk about it. I have a belief that talking about it sort of takes the place of DOING it."

    Brain check: Does this sound familiar in your case? Many would-be-achievers announce their goals so that others will applaud and give them pats on the back. Then, after they've gotten their praise without doing anything, they may feel a sense of letdown. They may feel, "What's the point of doing it?" You got your accolades up front for doing nothing but talking. How much higher can you go?

3. Years ago, whenever I had some prospects call to sign up for my services as a personal trainer, and they told me by phone they'd be in later to pay me, I'd immediately get on the horn and call a friend. I'd commence bragging about having just signed up some clients.

"That's incredible," my friend said, followed by, "Wow, that's awesome. Great."

When I hung up the phone something changed. It was as if I jinxed myself. When appointment time came around I was left to twiddle my thumbs. I waited and waited and waited. No new clients showed.

This same scenario played itself more times than I care to mention, until I finally broke this approval-seeking vice. When I curbed my urge to tell others how great I was doing before the results were etched in stone, future prospects who said they were coming by did drop by. And they paid. After they paid, if I kept my yap shut about it, more clients continued to flow to me.

Keeping quiet worked so well in my business that I used the same behavior in my martial arts training. Why tell anyone what I'm planning to do? Use the energy to train, not to talk.

Key metaphor to remember: When birds come to bathe in your bird-bath or eat from your feeder, if you talk too much they'll fly away. But if you observe, remain silent and let the energy build, even more birds will come.

When you've reached a level of mastery in setting and achieving goals, you can announce your intentions or goals to others, or you can still choose to refrain from doing so. Either way is fine because you now have the confidence that you'll follow through and get the job done no matter what.

Even so, you may be surprised at how much faster you work if you'll "zip the lips." Silence is golden.

The author reads a goal to himself at Temple of Heaven Park in Beijing, China.

7

The Power of One Move

"The power of one is above all things. The power to believe in yourself. Often well beyond any latent ability previously demonstrated. The mind is the athlete. The body is simply the means it uses."

– Bryce Courtenay

When I was a second-year collegiate wrestler, Eddie Banach, a 3-time NCAA champion (who also won Olympic Gold in 1984), watched closely as I lost a challenge match to an underclassman. For over a year Eddie witnessed my drive, determination and work ethic. And that may explain why he decided to take me aside and offer a bit of advice.

"You're doing a lot of great things out there," Eddie began. "You're trying a lot of different moves. And that's good. Even so, I'd like you to remember one thing: to become a national champion, all you need is one takedown that no one in the country can stop."

One takedown no one can stop? That's all it took? Why on earth did wrestling have hundreds and hundreds of moves and countermoves if it only took one good one to become a champion?

Although, on the surface, Eddie's advice may not appear to make sense, I believed him. And to this day I'm grateful to him for what he taught me. Why? Because I became a national champion, in western wrestling as well as in the Chinese art of shuaijiao kung fu, with this concept in mind. In fact, Eddie's advice, still alive and active in my mind, helped guide me to a world title in Beijing 14 years ago. It's helped me immensely in business as well. It's also helped me as a business and success coach.

Your Bread-n-Butter Move

There is no sport, no martial art or endeavor in which the "one move" principle doesn't hold true. Yes, you can and will have other tools and techniques along the way. But make no mistake about it, when push comes to shove and your bread needs some butter, you better have ONE perfect "go to" move.

If you've ever watched Mariano Rivera, the future Hall-of-Fame closer for the New York Yankees, you've watched pitching poetry in real time. You'll also know that Rivera, for the most part, has only one pitch: a cutter. Yet, for most of his career, it's rare that anyone can hit it.

In today's world many people make the mistake of trying to be a master of many things, all at the same time. Sorry, mastery doesn't work that way.

Mastery comes from working on one move, even when you're bad at it. You work through the errors and missteps until you get competent. Then you work it some more until you're good. Then you train it some more until you're very good. And this continues, virtually non-stop, as you pass through various levels of ability.

No Such Thing as Boredom

The average person is too concerned about boredom to become a master. Show him one move and he's already thinking about the next move. He hasn't even practiced the first skill and he wants the next.

Winners don't get bored practicing the "same old thing." To them, it's the same skill done differently, done better, done with a goal in mind.

In the sport of golf, the pro never thinks he doesn't need to work on his swing anymore. He never thinks he's mastered it, even when he has. Each and every day, he goes out and works on the same skill with the intention of producing better results.

As an Internet marketer, much of my success has come as a result of sending out daily emails, which you can subscribe to at **mattfurey.com** and **psycho-cybernetics.com**. Many of the world's top marketers refer to me as the "world's greatest email copywriter." More than any other marketing skill, email is my bread-n-butter move. There are many other marketing methods used on the Internet, but if they don't enhance the one move I do best, I don't use them.

Learning the next move in anything is not a bad idea. But keep in mind that you always want to be in the process of perfecting your one throw, your one pitch, your one swing and your one marketing skill that no one can stop, even if he knows it's coming.

8

Knock Down This Wall

*"A single conversation with a wise man is better
than ten years of study."*

— Chinese Proverb

Over 100 years ago in China, a young man wanted to learn kung fu. So he went to visit a Taoist master who was well-known for training many great martial artists. Upon meeting, the master asked the young man what style of kung fu he'd like to learn. Being unsophisticated about martial matters and the names of different styles, the young man replied: "I want to learn the most powerful style of kung fu."

The master nodded and began training the young man in an open meadow where a cold spring lay underground. The master instructed him in proper breathing and posture. He told him to pull the earth's magnetic energy through his body and direct it through his palms. Then he taught him how to use his imagination and his intention when he delivered a palm strike with the energy he collected. And that was it. One technique.

More is Better?

Meanwhile the master worked with many other students, teaching them various styles of kung fu, all of which contained many different punches, kicks and strikes.

As the others learned so much, the master's newest student did his best to ignore the others. He threw himself into his practice, training in earnest, morning, afternoon and night. Everyday, without fail, the new student stood in the same place, breathed deeply and called forth his internal powers with each palm strike. He never struck anything but thin air, but in his imagination he saw himself doing far more.

The Afternoon Break

During the day the master would give the young man a break to teach him calligraphy, music and other arts. Then it was back to work in the open field.

After one year of training the master noted that the ground in front of the student was beginning to get moist with water from the underground spring. After another year he noticed a puddle beginning to form. A year later, the puddle began turning into a lake. And each year afterward it rose even higher.

The young man had no clue what was happening to the earth before him. All he did was train. But the Taoist master understood and was very pleased.

Time to Go Home

10 years went by. The young man had trained in the same spot and the water from the spring was now deep enough for boats to fish in. At this point the Taoist master approached his ace student and with no warning whatsoever said: "Okay, training finished. You can go home now."

Understandably confused and upset, the young man stood up to the master: "What do you mean I can go home? I've been here ten years and you've showed me nothing. I see you teaching the other students many, many techniques, but ME, all you've had me do is stand in one place, breathe and punch the air."

The Taoist master smiled and said, "Young man, come with me."

The two walked through the temple grounds until they came upon a brick wall. The Taoist master then said, "Now get into your stance and begin breathing the way I taught you. And whenever you feel you're ready, strike this wall as hard as you can."

The student was not pleased with this request, but he got into his stance and began to pull the Earth's energy into his body. Then he struck the wall with his open palm. After doing so he immediately looked at the master as if to say, "Okay, now what?"

More Than Meets the Eye

But his questioning was abruptly interrupted by the wall disintegrating before him. As his eyes grew wide with wonder, his master looked at him and said, "And you said I taught you nothing? You came to learn the most powerful kung fu, and that is exactly what I taught you. Now you can see the power you have within you. What person can stand up to a strike as powerful as yours? Tell me, who have I trained in the other, fancier looking styles, who can stand up to you?"

The student bowed his head, thinking.

The master continued: "Take a look at the lake where you trained. Ten years ago there was nothing but an underground spring. Today the spring is overflowing. A lake is now in the meadow. So again, I tell you, your training is finished. You can go home now. Just remember that you have a responsibility to never use your power the wrong way."

Tears of Gratitude

The young man fell at the master's knees and began to weep. His tears were a combination of gratitude and sorrow.

Moral of the story: You get what you ask for. If you're willing to listen, learn and practice, one great technique practiced for years is far superior to a thousand techniques practiced over a weekend.

9

Suffer Now, Live it Up Later

"I hated every minute of training, but I said,
"Don't quit. Suffer now and live the rest of your life
as a champion.""

— Muhammad Ali

When I began in business in 1987, I painted a Muhammad Ali quote on the wall of my gym. It read as follows: "Suffer now and live the rest of your life as a champion."

Many of the clients I trained looked at the quote and got the message. Others didn't. The ones who got the message succeeded. The ones who believed they didn't need to suffer never got anywhere.

Suffering is a state of mind that you go through on your way to focused bliss. Think about the foregoing sentence for a moment.

What Ali Really Meant

I may be wrong, but I think I know what Ali meant when he said he hated every minute of the training. I don't think he "literally" meant what he said. I don't think he hated the training. Great martial artists and combat sports champions love to train. But there are moments when it hurts, and during those moments you hate the pain, but not enough to give in or give up.

So I believe what Ali meant was that when he wasn't focused on his goal, the training was hard. It was brutal. But as soon as he put his mind on the goal, he could handle it. He could bear it. He stopped suffering. He could now endure the training. He could keep going.

As a college wrestler, I discovered this truth during practices where my side ached in pain; when my sweats were dripping with perspiration; when my shoes were sopped and left a slosh mark with every step.

Many, many times I wanted to call it quits for the day. But a message came to me in the midst of my agony. "Furey, put your mind on your goal. What's your goal? Don't you want to be a national champion?"

Imagine Victory

When I shifted my mental focus I imagined getting my hand raised. I pictured being written up in the newspapers and interviewed on television. Within seconds of changing the pictures I was playing in my mind, the side ache was gone. The pain no longer existed and I continued onward in a state of reverie.

Best of all, by shifting my focus, when it came time for competition, an amazing thing happened: I won the tournament, got interviewed for the papers and made the nightly news.

Strange?

Not at all when you understand the power lying within your imagination. It's what connects you with the Universe and gives you the capacity to create what you want in life.

Here's a suggestion: Before and during your next workout, mentally pretend you are already at the finish line. See yourself celebrating being in possession of what you desire. During practice, when you're challenged to see how badly you want your goal, you may have a tendency to forget about the finish line. Yet the trick to creating is keeping your eyes on the prize while staying focused on what you're doing in the present moment.

Some goals come easier than others. Champions understand this. But the achievements champions prize more than anything, are the battles that test them with every fiber of their being.

Think about this today. Are you suffering in any way? If so, refocus on your goal and watch the pain dissipate. Keep doing this and you'll come to know the meaning of the phrase: "Suffer now and live the rest of your life as a CHAMPION."

Muhammad Ali used these words to become a world champion. What will you accomplish with them?

10

Excellence or Fun?

*"The secret of joy in work is contained in one word –
excellence. To know how to do something well
is to enjoy it."*

– Pearl S. Buck

One of the reasons we love sports and martial arts so much
is because they're two of the last models our society has left in which
excellence is encouraged and rewarded.

Both are activities in which it's okay to stand out, to rise up,
to be better than others, to earn more than your neighbor and be
applauded for it.

We love seeing a competitor rise above the others to become
great. We love finding out who the champion of a tournament is, who was
awarded the highest honors and who draws the biggest crowd or salary.

We also love to find out HOW the champion became who he or
she is. How did he train? What did he learn along the way that helped
him? What masters did he learn from?

The Rise and Fall of Fun

In many sports programs today, however, especially those
involving our youth, excellence is no longer being rewarded. Instead of

having a most valuable player award or a most inspirational award – EVERYONE is given a trophy, whether he truly earned one or not.

Several months ago, I cringed as I listened to a Little League baseball coach say to his team, "I don't care if you lose every game you play this year so long as you have fun. Having fun is what it's all about."

I couldn't believe what I was hearing, so I listened even closer. It was sad. Without realizing it, the coach took the bright light in those young eager eyes and made them go dim, all in the name of "fun."

"I don't want to see any crying, either," the coach continued. "If you strike out, I want you to run back to the dugout with a smile on your face."

Huh? How about channeling your anger in a positive direction? How about learning to wipe the slate clean and working to do better next time? But making a choice not to cry, at age 10? I've watched the pros cry in the dugout after losing a World Series. So how is it that a 10-year old should never cry?

It gets worse, though: "Now, one more thing," the coach said, if you guys can't make it to practice, no problem. Just tell me. It doesn't matter. We're going to have a lot of fun."

Four months later, when the season ended, no one on the team had much fun. The coaches included. The team went 2-14. They almost lived up to the expectation set for them at the outset. They almost lost every game they played.

What We Can Teach Our Children

Instead of "fun" being the gold-standard in youth sports, how about teaching the importance of practicing to become excellent? How about teaching them how to use their creative imagination, to visualize, to set goals, to study and practice every aspect of a martial art or sport?

It's not any more difficult to teach our youth to love the journey as well as the game, to teach them to accept victory with humility and class. It's also important to teach them to learn from mistakes with a calm perseverance.

But don't tell the youth of today that activity is only "for fun." You aren't fooling anyone with that line, especially the children. Deep down they know that we keep score for a reason, and that awards aren't supposed to go to everyone.

When I was a competitive swimmer, I won the Most Valuable Player (MVP) award two years in a row (age 12 and 13). The next year the coach discontinued the award, saying, "No one on our team is more valuable than anyone else. All of you are just as important as anyone else on the team."

Theoretically, she was partially correct. But, in reality, she didn't' want to give the trophy to me another time. Instead, she invented a new award for her younger sister, who was also on the team. I think it was the "I Love My Little Sister Award."

Is It Fair to Punish Success?

I continued to compete in swimming three more years after the coach made this move. I won all but a couple races in that time span, breaking records everywhere I competed. And at the end of the year, when the banquet was held, I applauded those who won awards.

I never received another award in the sport, despite my efforts, and that's probably why I eventually lost interest. This is tragic when you consider that while in college, Dale Henry, an assistant coach for the University of Iowa swimming team, saw me in the pool doing laps for my conditioning while recovering from an ankle sprain.

"Just for fun," he said, "I'd like to time you doing one lap of butterfly. Would that be okay with you?"

"Sure," I said, getting out of the pool. I walked to the starting blocks and took my mark. Coach Henry blew the whistle. I dove in and swam the length of the pool in seven strokes.

"That was 11 seconds," he said. "Could you come into my office for a few minutes? I'd like to speak to you."

"Okay."

Never Stop Learning

As I sat next to Coach Henry's desk, he told me the following: "Matt, you have the potential to swim a 47 flat 100-meter butterfly. If you ever decide you'd rather swim instead of wrestle, come see me and I'll find a place for you on the team."

Outside his office the Big Ten records were posted on the wall. I looked out at them and saw the following record posted: 100-Fly – Mark Spitz, Indiana, 1971, 47:00.

Although I stuck with wrestling and later gravitated to the study of Chinese martial arts, I will always wonder how well I would have done if I chose swimming over wrestling. I stuck with wrestling because I loved it, was intrigued by it and never stopped learning how I could get better.

I'm all for giving every kid a certificate or trophy if that makes each athlete feel good, but there's still room for an MVP trophy, a Most Improved trophy and a Most Inspirational trophy.

Make a bigger trophy and a separate award for the boys and girls who do better than the rest. If it's good enough for the Big Leagues, then it's good enough for our youth.

Make sports and martial arts fun – but emphasize that in the real world, becoming excellent at something is a whole lot more fun than being lousy.

Excellence is Fun Turned Inside-Out

Build your child's self-image with activities that challenge his or her athleticism. Teach the value of practice. And regardless of whether your child becomes a champion or not, you can show him how much he improved by using his mind and body in the right way.

Tell a child that it's only "for fun" and he'll never learn the value of practice and what can be accomplished because of it.

Sports and martial arts are two of the last remaining activities that haven't been collectivized with the "not everyone can be great, so let's punish the best among us and make everyone the same" ideology.

At least not yet. Heaven help us if that ever happens.

The author exercising in Xinjiang Province, China.

11

What You Picture in Your Mind Matters

"The winners in life think constantly in terms of I can, I will, and I am. Losers, on the other hand, concentrate their waking thoughts on what they should have or would have done, or what they can't do."

– Dennis Waitley

What are you picturing before lopping off to sleep at night? What are you thinking about first thing in the morning, when your eyes open? Are your mental pictures mega powerful, so-so or weak? I ask these questions because when you go to bed and wake up, your mind is preparing a map to navigate through your day.

The average person is totally unconscious about what he thinks about during these important moments, as well as many other peak moments each day. The superior person is not. He knows what he wants and his thoughts reflect it.

What you are picturing and saying to yourself when you arise each morning sets the tone for how you will feel and what results you will get for the rest of the day. The same goes for what you are imagining before you go to bed at night. What you are pondering before bed influences what you will dream about. It even sets the tone for how you will feel when you wake up the next day.

Tired or Energized?

You can go to bed with the words, 'I'm tired' playing in your head. If you do, chances are excellent you'll wake up eight or so hours later and you still won't be refreshed. Subconsciously this final thought caused 'I'm tired' to play all night long. In a sense it programmed your mental computer to wake up in the same state you went to bed.

Now, if you were to experiment with a different thought like, "Tomorrow I will wake up feeling energized" – I think you'll be amazed at what happens. I'm willing to bet you'll wake up filled with energy, enthusiasm and pizzazz. I've taught this technique for years and when people are willing to try it they're usually astounded at how fast it works.

Smiling Encounter or Rough Meeting?

Let's think about how this exercise applies to your job, your training or how you mentally prepare for competition. Let's say you have a tough meeting tomorrow and you need to talk to someone who is really arrogant. How are you going to picture this meeting? What are you going to say to get yourself ready? Moreover, what would happen if you started picturing yourself and the other person as smiling and getting along, able to easily communicate with each other? I'm willing to bet this mental picture will greatly influence the outcome.

Now, if you think this way and see yourself getting along in your meeting, I can assure you that everything will go a lot smoother for you. Will it go perfectly? I doubt it. But when all is finished, it'll feel perfect compared to what you were thinking previously.

Ideally, you don't want to always be repeating the same old history that doesn't work. You want to create a new series of positive moments and experiences.

What Kind of History Do You Want to Repeat?

You can stop repeating the kind of history you don't want right now. You can do so by continually picturing the way you get along in meetings or elsewhere when you're at your best. If you see yourself at your best, you'll be at your best more often.

Mentally review your best practices, your best moments, best meeting, best encounters and best experiences. Recall the days when everything worked like magic. If you'll do this, you'll start having a lot more "best" days, and you'll do so with an uncanny frequency.

"Imagination is the Elixir of Life"

P.T. Barnum once said, "Imagination is the elixir of life." Play negative movies in your mind and you create a toxic solution. Play positive movies in your imagination and you'll have an elixir that causes you to instantly stand up straighter, breathe more fully and move forward with a smile on your face.

To change the results you're getting you must change how you feel, and how you feel is based on how you picture things in your mind. How you picture things will either open you to life's possibilities or chain you to a life of self-imposed limitations.

Upgrade your mental movies. Play the best you have. Do this everyday and more of 'the best' will come your way.

12

2 Kinds of Pride

*"The fall from the ladder of success is a lot quicker
than the climb up."*

– Pete Lillo

There are two types of pride. One is essential to your success; the other a harbinger of doom. From a positive sense, pride connotes self-respect or dignity. You have a healthy attitude about who you are and what you've accomplished. This is the disposition needed to navigate toward and achieve your goals.

Healthy Pride

"Healthy" does not mean displaying a smug or gloating facial expression or nose-in-the-air haughtiness. Healthy pride often appears in the form of gratitude for what you've accomplished. It's usually accompanied by realizing that as humans we are prone to mistakes and failure. It's knowing how a fine line separates a winning state of mind from a loser's mentality. It's understanding, as my friend Pete Lillo once told me, "The fall from the ladder of success is a lot quicker than the climb up."

One of the quickest ways of losing your step is to think only about how great you are. Instead of remembering and acknowledging those who helped you along the way, you think you are one hundred percent self-created.

Sports, martial arts and business are filled with people with unhealthy pride. At first, an athlete listens and learns. But once he accomplishes something major or becomes a champion, his disposition can do an about face. After he wins, he becomes someone else. It's almost as if he has become infected with "masteritis" or "championitis?"

The sickness is major, but the antidote is simple. Here it is:

The Cure for Unhealthy Pride

- Don't celebrate to excess

- Don't think you are a better human being than others just because you have developed a skill to a higher degree than they have

- Don't believe you are smarter than the coaches and mentors you've had or the books and courses you've studied

Recognize Your Help

Realize you had guidance up the ladder of success. You wouldn't have reached the first rung on your own.

This is tough advice for intellectuals or those who've experienced a good share of success, especially if they were inundated with praise after an accomplishment of great magnitude.

Keeping your sense of pride on the healthy side of the fence can be difficult, especially if you perform before a crowd. You are vulnerable to the wrong kind of pride whenever you succeed before a large crowd of people, and in the aftermath of success, you are lauded with praise.

It takes exceptional character to accept the praise, but redirect the energy toward self-improvement. Failure to recirculate the praise dooms many whom otherwise would have gone on to succeed. Anyone with an "I'm where I am because of me and me alone" attitude is destined for disappointment. Yes, you are a key part of your success equation, but no one succeeds alone.

Without Dr. Daniel Weng's guidance I would not have won a world shuaijiao kung fu title. He taught me simple movements that created big gaps in my opponents' defenses. Same goes for all my college wrestling coaches. I could not have excelled without their help.

Granted, celebrating after a victory feels wonderful. It's also important. But equally important is immediately setting another goal; one that keeps your mind focused on the reality that success is an ongoing journey, not a final resting place.

Use your previous successes as stepping-stones to a brighter future. View your previous victories and the energy they contain to spur you on to greater accomplishments, but don't for one moment think your winning moments are because of YOU and you alone. Anyone who gets to the top doesn't just land there. He has help all along the way.

13

Tough Times Never Last

"Always look at what you have left. Never look at what you have lost."

– Robert H. Schuller

In 1987, when I was starting in business, I had a copy of Dr. Robert Schuller's ***Tough Times Never Last But Tough People Do*** on my desk. 'Twas an important book for me to be reading at the time because I faced a number of serious challenges. And one of those challenges was figuring out how to make enough money to pay my bills and put food on my table.

There were many moments when all seemed hopeless. The phone wasn't ringing. No one was responding to my ads and I was very close to being out of business.

A few times I sunk so low I began to ponder the unthinkable: Being out on the street, begging for food. Instead of figuring out what I needed to do to get more business, at times I would read the classified ads, wondering who could give me a job.

Three of the keys that carried me out of the tough times were books, positive mental movies and an attitude of gratitude. Let me explain each in detail:

1. **Books –** *Tough Times Never Last But Tough People Do* got me to realize that I wasn't alone and the tough times weren't going to stay with me. Another book, **Psycho-Cybernetics**, taught me how to build my confidence and improve my self-image by reliving positive experiences from the past. It taught me how my mistakes, setbacks and failures weren't negatives. Instead they were corrective feedback helping me to achieve the goals I set for myself.

2. **Positive mental movies –** When I speak of positive mental movies I don't mean visualizing the future. First, I mean remembering your positive past. The moments when everything was in flow. The times when you were at your best. Recalling these moments makes it easy to realize that more positive experiences are on the way. Second, because we remember with the same part of our brain in which we visualize the future, when we recall previous victories our mind opens to receive more.

3. **Gratitude –** When you sink to an all-new emotional low, you're in a perfect position to climb out of it. And the way out is finding anything for which you can be grateful. If you're down to your last nickel, instead of crying about what you lost or what could have been, you give thanks for the one nickel you still have. Then you look for more things to praise. The clothes on your back, the skin on your frame, your eyesight, hearing, sense of smell and taste. You look for anything you can to pull yourself out of the abyss. Gratitude is like a rope dropped from the heavens to pull you out of a downward current.

To some, the above may appear as if it couldn't possibly change your circumstances. Yet, if you were to interview a few dozen failures who became successful, I'd bet the majority would agree to having practiced these keys in one form or another.

Successful people leave footprints. They leave clues. They leave ways for us to move beyond our troubles and become the person we want to be.

If you're struggling right now, keep these three keys in mind. Spend time each day counting your blessings. This alone can cause a miraculous turnaround. Continue to read inspiring books of heroism and conquest. Make a list of a dozen positive experiences from your past, no matter how long ago, no matter how insignificant they may seem to you right now. Memories of victories are very important in helping you bridge the gap from frustration and failure to elated celebration.

It's always far easier to think about our defeats, setbacks, failures and frustrations. But if you do this too often, you give these experiences encouragement. You unknowingly tell your subconscious that you'd like more of them.

On the other hand, when you recall and relive your positive past, you tell your subconscious mind to direct you toward more of the same.

When times are tough, remember that tough times never last. But tough people do.

14

The Biggest Competitor You Will Ever Face

"The greatest champions in sports are those who make themselves their greatest opponent."

– Jim Furey (Dad)

Competition is a good thing. A great thing. It brings out the best in a person. It shines a light on a person's true weaknesses.

Yet, after a competition, or even a tough practice, there is a danger for the person who gets beat, as well as the person who does well. On one hand, the person who loses may consider himself a failure and begin to lose confidence. On the other, the person who wins may think he's better than he is, that he no longer needs instruction or needs to keep learning.

It is one thing to say to yourself: *I didn't do well today, but I'll do better next time. I wasn't myself today. I didn't win today, but I'm still a winner inside. I believe in myself and I'll prove that I can rise above this.*

It's quite another to think: *I'm the best so I don't need to practice like I did before.*

Overcoming Defeat

Sure, the sting of defeat can be difficult to overcome, especially if you really wanted to win. But you must transcend the sting if you expect to move to the next level.

The best athletes and martial artists don't compete with others as much as they compete with themselves. Even when they win they stay connected to their vision of "constant improvement." Eventually their constant improvements lead to mastery, and mastery is understanding that the goal and the journey are linked in a circular chain. You work toward what you want while seeing the process of achieving the goal as a journey. And when you achieve your goal you move to the next link on the chain.

Work Toward Your Goal

You train day after day, no matter what. Your first day of training, as well as your 1,000th and 10,000th, is all the same; they're all part of the same circular chain known as the master's ongoing journey.

A master knows that although competition stimulates him to become better, ultimately, he is his greatest competition. Victory is not so much winning against others as it is winning the game with yourself. It's not winning "over" yourself, but winning "with" yourself. Getting into harmony with your body, mind and soul.

Now, once you are better than all your competitors, you might wonder how you can continue to improve if your focus is simply about beating everyone else. My father gave me the answer when I was in college. He told me how the greatest champions of all times are those who "make themselves their greatest opponent." He was right.

Remember the Feeling

In order to make yourself your greatest competition, you use memory-power. You go back in time and picture your best moments, your greatest successes. You relive the feelings of confidence you experienced.

The author with his son and daughter in New York's Central Park.

Doing so is the same as a good friend reminding you of your value; how you're someone special. The only difference is now you are being a good friend to yourself. You're digging deep and finding the BIG SELF within, the part of yourself who inherently knows you came into this world to succeed, not to fail.

I once knew a businessman who'd been successful for more than ten years. Then the demand for his product died off and he had to close up shop. He thought of himself as a failure.

I talked to the man and said, "My goodness, you had 10 years of success. I wouldn't call that a failure. Remember the successful days of the business and close the chapter your reading on failure. Figure out a way to tap into another current trend and you'll be off to the races once again."

He listened and in short order he was succeeding in another business. Some businesses stay alive a long time. Others die young. Then there are those who have a good run for 10 or more years. Either way, you'll never get better by reliving memories from the "bad old days." Remember the best times and move forward with the idea of creating more of them.

There are great athletes who go undefeated until the **big show**. Then, if they lose the championship, they feel like failures. They're not. They simply lost one game. They won almost **all** of their games. This is what they need to focus on in the present to improve their future. They need to keep replaying the games they won and discover **why** they won them. When this is done, you bring your previous success experiences into the finals with you. Remembering your success experiences increases the odds that you'll succeed again in the future. Reliving mistakes, not for the sake of learning, but to beat yourself up, causes you to create more failures. Which would you rather do? Create more success or more failure?

Assuming you chose success, remember this: No matter what you are doing, picture what you want and give it everything you have and the final score will take care of itself. Make yourself your greatest competition and you'll be leaving everyone else you used to compete against in the dust. It's the way of the champion.

15

Competence vs. Confidence

"Whatever we expect with confidence becomes our own self-fulfilling prophecy."

– Brian Tracy

Someone once told me that being competent in a skill is more important than having confidence in it. I disagree.

Why? Because the world is filled with competent people who don't believe in themselves. They're on every corner of the globe; they're on every street corner, in every classroom and business.

In every sport or martial art I can think of, if all you have is competence, you may be in for a serious beating. You need confidence as well as competence.

Mental Mistakes

Here's a truth I've seen played out again and again. If you are highly skilled but lack confidence, you'll be passive when it's time to be aggressive. Or you'll be aggressive when you'd be better off being a bit passive. In short, you'll use the wrong strategy at the worst possible time. You'll make mental mistakes.

There would be many highly skilled champions in the making *if* they only had the confidence to stick with their training, day in and day out, until they mastered their sport; if they only knew how to inject instantaneous confidence into their mind and body when they needed it most.

Becoming competent in anything requires a certain amount of confidence. It requires a belief in yourself that positively affects everything about you; a belief that is so strong other people pick up on it and begin to believe in you, too.

Embrace the Struggle

I recently spoke with a man who struggled for years to learn the art of archery. At first it was incredibly difficult for him compared to others in his class. But he never quit on himself or the art. He kept at it even when he felt like he was making no progress, and today, while so many of the others who were ahead of him in the beginning have quit, he's still practicing. Today, he's competent as well as confident. He hung in long enough to acquire both attributes.

Keep this in mind: Even when you're competent, you still need to project confidence in what you are competent in. If you don't, your high level of competence will not be taken seriously by anyone, yourself included.

But when you're confident in learning the things you're not competent in, you will surprise yourself and others at how much faster you learn. The person who KNOWS he can learn whatever he sets his mind on has an edge over the person who doubts himself.

Many people who are successful in one area of their life won't venture into new arenas because they believe they lack confidence. A few years ago I talked to a man who made over a million dollars per year for 10-straight years. Even so, he was tired of his job and all the stress he endured. He wanted to get started in the information marketing business and confessed to me: "I'd like to learn how to write books, put up websites and create videos, BUT I don't have ANY confidence."

I replied: *"How can you not have ANY confidence? Everyone has confidence. You just don't know where you put it. Let me reintroduce you to the part of yourself who knows how to succeed."*

You'll instantly know how to do this yourself if you'll take the time to remember a segment of your life in which you were confident. It could be speaking a foreign language; it might even be something as simple as walking.

Have Confidence

At one time you were neither competent nor confident in the skill you now perform with ease. But now you are confident in this area. This means you HAVE confidence. You just don't know how to transfer the energy in that mental movie to other areas of interest.

You're in good hands when you find the movie in your mind labeled "CONFIDENCE." Once you find it, begin breathing, picturing and moving the way you would if you were doing the thing you are confident in. Then keep breathing and moving the same way you would move if you were already confident?

What did you discover? If you're honest, you'll note that you increased your confidence and competence by moving and acting the way you do in the area you already have confidence.

I remember when I began studying Chinese. At first I was frustrated with my inability to pronounce the words, much less hear and express the various tones. I thought to myself, *"Man, I'm an idiot. The other people in the class are learning so much faster than I am. I don't get it. I can't learn this. It's too hard."*

Overcoming Doubts

These negative self-talk statements showed a lack of confidence in what I was doing. How did I overcome them? By remembering that I couldn't speak English very well when I got started as an infant. By remembering how I couldn't dress myself, tie my shoes or feed myself.

By remembering I was a lousy swimmer, couldn't hit or catch a baseball; that I couldn't read or write.

Everything I can now do, I was unable to do at one time. Yet, through the process of making mistakes and using the feedback from those mistakes, I was able to learn everything I set my mind on learning. On the other hand, in all the areas where I gave up on myself, guess what happened? I never got better in those areas.

One day last year, when I was thinking about the importance of confidence, I stumbled upon an old negative memory from 2nd grade art class. I caught myself saying something I'd repeated for years.

"I can't draw. I'm a lousy artist. I can barely draw stick figures, much less anything else."

These lines weren't anything new. I'd been repeating them to myself for 40 years. As a result of this repetition, guess how much my artwork had evolved over the years?

"Not at all" would be the correct answer.

When I got hold of this thinking pattern, I immediately searched my mind for any positive memories I might have about drawing. To my surprise I found one. In the process of studying Mandarin, I learned to draw Chinese characters. I then said to myself, "If I can learn to draw Chinese characters, I can learn to draw."

Minutes later I wrote my friend, Vince Palko, a cartoonist who did all the artwork in my book, **Combat Conditioning**. I told him what I discovered about myself in relation to art. And I asked if he would teach me. Vince immediately agreed. He was excited to help me overcome my 2nd grade hurdle.

When Vince showed up to begin our first lesson, I'll admit being uneasy. I felt like I was setting myself up for failure. But when I realized I'm not trying to be Picasso or Van Gogh, that I just wanted to be able to draw well enough to say, with confidence, "Hey, I can draw" – I settled down, relaxed and began learning.

Today, I can draw A LOT more than stick figures. In fact, when I teach seminars and conduct trainings, I often use a white board to illustrate what I'm teaching. When I draw on the white board, no one ever says, "Dude, you can't draw." Especially me.

I now believe I can draw. The belief started to take hold of me when I realized that drawing wasn't much different than learning to write Chinese characters. All I needed was an opening in my mind. This opening appeared when I looked at what I could already do – not what I thought I was incapable of doing.

When I recalled something from the past that I once struggled with but can now perform well, I was able to flip the switch and install confidence in a new area. All I had to do was remember competence will take some time, just as it does in anything. It all boils down to practice.

How long did the switch take? A few seconds. Did the switch give me instant competence? No. But it did give me the confidence to stick with the job until I became competent.

All musicians who learn to play an instrument start out playing poorly. But if they continue to practice and persevere, they will find a way to cut through the frustration and play beautiful music. Whether they play as well in concert as they do in practice will be a matter of confidence.

There are great practice fighters who appear flawless while training. But when the competition is REAL, they find a way to lose. Why? It's not lack of competence. They know what to do. They just don't do it when it matters most.

Think competence is more important than confidence? Think again. Both attributes are important, but only one of them gives you wings.

16

Breathe More – Do More

"Winning is the most important thing in my life, after breathing. Breathing first, winning next."

– George Steinbrenner

Most people get it all wrong when it comes to being in superior condition. They think the key to being in great shape is long distance running, or long distance biking, or some other long, slow distance "aerobic" activity.

This is not the case.

The first key to great cardio is doing the opposite of what you've been told. If you're doing an exercise that does NOT force you to lose your breath – typically considered anaerobic exercise – then you're not forcing your heart and lungs to make a major adaptation, and major adaptation is what creates great cardiovascular fitness.

"Lost Secrets"

Ever been told that sprints are not "aerobic" because you're not using oxygen? HELLO.

When you do a hill sprint, you're using FAR more oxygen, far faster, than if you go for a jog around the block. This is why hill sprints are one of the "lost secrets" of burning off excess flab in record time.

The author running hills in New Zealand.

You generate so much oxygen that you blow the toxins out your lungs, much like taking your new Ferrari (or Mini-Cooper) out for a spin on the freeway. You open the engine and let it roar.

That's REAL cardio. But if you only drove the sports car around town at 25 mph, that would be akin to long-distance cardio. It's okay, but what your body really needs is a KICK into high gear. That's how it gets stronger.

The second key to being in great condition is doing bodyweight exercises like those I teach in my best-seller, **Combat Conditioning** – (available at **MattFurey.com**).

Bodyweight exercises, such as Hindu pushups and Hindu squats work the major muscle groups and get you breathing deeply. Deep breathing forces your body to get stronger, to melt excess fat from your body and to dramatically increase your energy level.

Eat Right

The third key to being in great condition is getting off all the processed foods that weigh you down and steal your body's energy. Sugary snacks, pizza, crackers, pastries, for example, are not good for you. They're rough on the system. They elevate blood sugar levels. They make you fat, sluggish and slow.

Many starchy high-fat foods have helped turn 20 million Americans into diabetics. Another 41 million have been diagnosed as PRE-diabetic. What's worse, the 41 million people figure only represents the ones who have been diagnosed. Millions more have yet to see the doctor.

Accelerators of the aging process are substances like sugar and high fructose corn syrup. If you're junking out on cola drinks, pastries and candy, you're having temporary fun at the expense of long-time health.

As a former collegiate wrestler, I had to regularly drop a load of water weight within 24 hours of competition. I found the cleaner my diet, the easier it was to break a sweat and reduce my weight. On the other hand, if I was eating sugar or drinking it in the form of soft drinks, cutting water weight was a nightmare. Sugar kills – plain and simple. And for many people, starchy carbohydrates are just as bad as plain old sugar.

Key number four: Pay heed to the words of **Chuang Tzu**, who said, *"Ordinary people breathe from their throats; extraordinary people breathe from their feet."*

Each day, even when you're not training, you are training. You're exercising your breath. You're breathing deeply and keeping your energy levels high so you can do more in a spirit of calm.

To practice deep breathing exercises or **chi kung**, sit on the edge of a chair with your back straight. Or stand with your feet a shoulder-width apart. Let your shoulders relax. Tuck in your pelvis to remove the curve from your lower back. Let your whole body relax. Inhale through your nose and imagine your lungs extend all the way to the space beneath your feet. Gently pull the inhale all the way to your feet, then exhale slowly through your nose. Repeat for three breaths and note how much better you feel. Then repeat for several minutes and observe an even bigger change in your mental state. See how quickly you go from stressed out to calm and centered.

Follow these keys and you'll quickly see how much more energy you have to get more done in less time. Breath more – do more.

17

The Legs Feed the Wolf

"We should be dreaming. We grew up as kids having dreams, but now we're too sophisticated as adults, as a nation. We stopped dreaming. We should always have dreams."

— Herb Brooks

I recently watched a segment from the movie **Miracle**. It's about the 1980 U.S. Olympic Hockey team, who did the unthinkable; defeating the juggernaut Soviet team on the way to Olympic gold.

The segment I watched was when head coach Herb Brooks had the team skating wind sprints immediately after a lackluster game in Sweden. During the game the athletes were staring off into the stands, pointing out the "hot" women seated in various rows. Coach Brooks silently took note of the team's lack of focus, and corrected it by nearly running them to death.

As I watched I yearned for more, so I purchased the DVD and had it sent by overnight mail. The next day I sat and watched the entire movie (it's 2.5 hours long) with my son. We watched it again the next day. And I'm certain we'll be watching it over and over again. It's that powerful.

Get Used to This Drill

One of the most important lines in the movie is when the men are doing sprints at the end of practice. As they burst across the ice on their skates, Coach Brooks tells everyone they better get used to this drill. Later on he hollers, "The legs feed the wolf." When I heard this I pushed the rewind button and played it again. And again. Then I took out a pen and wrote it in my journal.

A couple days later, I was still thinking about the phrase and its meaning. Like coaches I have had throughout my career, including Dan Gable and Karl Gotch, Herb Brooks was obsessed with conditioning. To him, "the legs feed the wolf" meant that great hockey players, like wolves on the hunt, need speed and endurance. Not either-or. Both.

"Conditioning is Your Best Hold"

Karl Gotch referred to conditioning as "your best hold." Gable was fanatical about conditioning as well. But neither had a line as good as Brooks' "the legs feed the wolf."

I have a couple other ways of explaining the benefits of "the legs feed the wolf." One is that sprints or speed-endurance work triggers your body to release more yang energy. When you sprint, you not only get faster and generate more endurance, you also turn back the clock and cause your body to get younger. Sprinting causes your body to naturally secrete more HGH and testosterone, whereas long-distance cardio causes the opposite reaction. The key is sprint-rest, sprint-rest, sprint-rest. Take 30 seconds to two minutes between bursts, then do another. As soon as your lungs recover, do another one.

Another way I look at "the legs feed the wolf" involves a slight word variation. By changing the word 'wolf' to 'will' we have even more meaning.

Strong Legs Equals Strong Will

"The legs feed the will." What does this mean? Well, when you sprint you cause the lungs, the kidneys and the heart to get stronger. You adapt or die. And when the organs of the body are strengthened, so are the muscles.

Sprinting causes your kidneys to get stronger. If someone is weak-willed, his kidneys are weak. If he is strong-willed, his kidneys serve him well.

Strong legs not only feed the wolf, they also feed the will. It takes a strong will to run sprint after sprint when your lungs are dying for a break.

"The legs feed the wolf."

"The legs feed the will."

Either way you choose to see it, sprints give your body-mind the energy of champions.

18

90 Days of Non-stop Walking

"Nature arms each man with some faculty which enables
him to do easily some feat impossible to any other."

– Ralph Waldo Emerson

Ever miss a day of sleep? Ever go a couple nights without getting any rest?

No matter how uncomfortable you might feel from not sleeping for a night or two, it's nothing compared to going for a 90-day walk in which you're not allowed to sleep, sit or lie down.

Sounds crazy, I know. You'd have to be a modern day Superman to pull it off, right?

Well, there's a group of Tendai Buddhist monks in Japan who do the seemingly impossible. They're called Marathon monks and they live on Mt. Hiei near Kyoto.

Human Dynamos

Unlike other monks who are more meditative than physical, these monks are human dynamos who combine body and mind in all they do. All members of this sect must do one marathon per day for 100-straight days, through the rugged mountains, as part of their training.

Out of the entire lot of monks, a small and elite class are given the task of completing 1,000 marathons in seven years. And whoever finishes this feat is considered a Living Buddha or saint.

Since 1885, only 46 monks have survived the 1,000-marathons-in-seven-years-challenge. And I recently met one of them. His given name is Sakai Yusai. He's an 82-year old enlightened being who is affectionately referred to as **Ajari-san**, the Sanskrit word for guide.

Ajari-san became a monk at age 39 after his wife committed suicide and his mother-in-law was trying to drive him insane. In order to escape her wrath, he ran away to a monastery, where she couldn't get to him. Little did he know that the monks at this humble monastery would transform his life and make him a positive role model for the world to behold.

Ajari-san would normally be famous for completing the challenge of 1,000 marathons in seven years. But his fame transcends the event because he's the only monk who chose to do it twice. After the first round, he wasn't satisfied with how he did, even though it gave him Buddha status. He felt he could do better, and so he was allowed to run through the mountains of Mt. Hiei for another 1,000 marathons. Ajari-san must have known what he was capable of when he made the request because this time he completed the challenge in six years.

Now, just so you know, the 1,000 marathons challenge follows the Bushido code. This means you complete the ordeal or agree to take your own life. What this means is that on each and every day that Ajari-san would go out to run the mountain, he left his quarters dressed in white garments (signifying the color of death). Upon his feet he wore thin sandals made from rice. And inside his robe he carried a knife and white handkerchief; these served as a nudge, reminding him of his fate if he were to give up.

Sakai Yusai with the author, in Kyoto, Japan.

Incredible Feat

Not only is Sakai Yusai one of only two monks to do the 1,000 marathons twice – but he also performed the incredible feat of walking for 90-straight days.

No, I did not say he walked for an hour each day for 90-straight days.

Ajari-san walked, without sleep, for 90-straight days. Never allowed to sit. Never allowed to lie down. His only rest was the two meals he got per day, which he had to eat while STANDING.

As if this wasn't enough, after doing 700 of the 1,000 marathons, he underwent a 9-day fast with no food, no water and no sleep.

And just to make sure he wasn't too proud of himself after he completed his 1,000th marathon, he had to go through a seven-day fast while meditating before a large fire. Again, no food, no water and no sleep as he placed peoples' prayer petitions into the fire and chanted blessings for them.

In the Western world, people tend to think of mental and spiritual power as separate from the physical. The very notion is ludicrous. I don't believe you can reach the highest levels of mental and spiritual power without being physically active. Neither does Ajari-san.

Martial arts masters are wonderful examples of physical, mental and spiritual power. They perform amazing feats that defy logic. They master stunts that the average and ordinary cannot fathom. They also understand how everything they have done can be duplicated, if the spirit is willing and the flesh is strong.

If your spirit is willing but your flesh is weak – then you have no power. True power comes when both are strong. True power comes when you get behind your desires and stick with them, even when it hurts.

I put the accomplishments of Ajari-san head-and-shoulders above anything I have ever read or witnessed about an able-bodied person. You try walking without sleep for one day, much less 90, and I think you'll understand why I believe what I do. You try doing one marathon through the mountains, not to mention 1,000 in seven years and you'll get the picture.

If you ever begin feeling wimpy or weak, examples of masters like Ajari-san will help keep you going. Whatever you're doing is pretty simple and ordinary in comparison.

19

It's A Secret to You

"Isn't it astonishing that all these secrets have been preserved for so many years just so we could discover them!"

– Orville Wright

In China there is a kung fu master who is the heir of a lineage that no one else in the country knows. Liu is his name and the unique form of Taoist martial training he began learning as a child develops internal power like nothing I have ever seen.

Liu is 53 years young and is free of a single wrinkle on his face or age spot upon his skin. He doesn't look a day over 35. His muscles are solid with no excess fat or loose skin hanging. Even though Master Liu has never lifted weights in his entire life, at 170 pounds, he possesses a functional strength that would be hard to match.

Master Liu grew up in a small village in Henan Province, home of the world famous Shaolin Temple. When he was only eight years old, Liu's teacher began to pass his lineage on to him. And Liu has practiced it daily ever since. In fact, this particular lineage has been passed from one master to one student for over 2,000 years, making possession of the knowledge sacred.

Minutes after meeting Master Liu we went to an open area to begin training. To demonstrate his ability he grabbed my hand and motioned for me to punch him in the groin. After doing so he put his arms behind his back, spread his legs and asked me to kick him in the testicles as hard as I could. I kicked him several times. When I finished he smiled and gave me the thumbs-up sign. All of this is on film.

"Eat Bitter"

During my trips to China (where I have a vacation home), I spend a lot of time training with Master Liu. We train in the hot sun as well as the cool breeze later at night. He pushes me in each workout, telling me to "eat bitter."

After training the forms of this art and being drenched in sweat, Master Liu teaches me the applications of this ancient form. More than once he's knocked me further with less effort than anyone I have ever trained with in my life. Every strike, every push, every seemingly innocent movement can be turned into a death blow.

Before training with Master Liu I had heard how he'd fought 64 men in a row and no one lasted more than a few seconds. Such stories sound ridiculous to most people; they did to me as well, before I met him. After experiencing his power, I can tell you, I think if you ever needed someone to "mow down" a large group, Master Liu is the guy you'd pick to do the job for you.

When I train with him I discover, beyond all shadows of doubt, how fragile the human body is. At times, especially when we're in a peak emotional state, we may feel like we're made of iron. Yet, at any moment, a moment in which we may get injured or incur an illness, we wonder how we got out of balance so easily.

Health Signs

Master Liu doesn't just watch your form when you train, he also looks at your skin as well as how you sweat. Both are important indicators giving you information about the health of your entire body.

Got freckles or brown age-related spots? Master Liu tells you to practice the form and get rid of them. When you perspire, do your legs

The author with Master Liu, in China.

sweat as much as your upper body? If not, you need to practice more in order to open the meridians to greater chi flow.

"When you follow this system of kung fu, inside of a few months the old-age freckles will be gone," Master Liu said. "At age 70 and 80 you'll look the same as you do at 30 or 40. And you'll be just as strong. You don't get weaker as you age unless you're doing exercises that aren't powerful enough."

From time to time I have had someone tell me how he is much younger than his years. Invariably, when I meet the man in person I don't agree with his self-assessment. This is not the case with Master Liu. He's incredibly youthful in his appearance – as well as in terms of what he can do. He has, as Mark Twain would say, "The quiet confidence of a Christian with four Aces."

"I'm the only one in China who knows this form," said Master Liu. It was passed onto me by my teacher who had it passed to him. For over 2,000 years it has only been taught to one descendant. Now I am allowed to teach this form to others and help spread it."

"When you know this form your body becomes powerful inside as well as out. Someone can beat you with all his might and you'll feel no pain."

To prove his point further, Master Liu made his fist into a club and began to hit himself in soft areas of the body that offer no protection. He clubbed himself in the nose with full force several times. Nothing happened. Then he punched himself in the throat. Again, no pain.

This was no magic trick. This was real life.

There are some high-level performers who claim, "There are no secrets. The key to success is nothing but hard work."

In a sense, they're right. Then again, they're wrong.

Why do I say this? Because I've been coached by some of the greatest masters who've ever lived. And in China alone, I am continually amazed at the amount of truly secret knowledge that no one else has a hold of yet. Maybe someone somewhere knows a few of the things Master Liu knows; but I haven't met the person who truly understands everything he knows. This means that for most of the world, what Master Liu knows is truly "secret."

20

Backward Training

"One of the advantages of being disorderly is that one is constantly making exciting discoveries."

– A. A. Milne

It was the summer of 1984. The summer Olympics were in Los Angeles and I was working a wrestling camp in Cedar Falls, Iowa. The director of the camp, J Robinson, a former assistant to Dan Gable at the University of Iowa, was soon to take over the University of Minnesota program and turn them into national champions.

Robinson was a great coach and an incredible technician on the mat, who taught me a great deal. But he was no one to model when it came to injuries.

He was only 40 at the time of that camp and his body was quite literally beat to hell. He'd been through so many knee operations that he could pop his knee in and out of socket with ease. I'll never forget the day I heard J brag to another wrestler about the orthopaedic results he just received from the University of Iowa hospital. "Look at me," J said. "I'm 63% disabled and I can still whoop ass."

Never Complained

To his credit, despite the immense and oftentimes intense pain J had on a daily basis, he never quit working. And he never complained.

The author practicing backward in Japan.

Plus, he was always ripe for a challenge. So no one was shocked on that hot, humid July afternoon in 1984, when J and his good friend, Norm Wilkerson, shook hands on a bet.

What was the bet? Wilkie bet that he could run a 40-yard sprint faster backward than J could forward. This was a great bet when you considered that J had trouble walking from time to time. So no one figured it would even be a close race – except J.

The men marked their calendars. Twenty-one days into the camp they would have their BIG RACE.

Leading up to the event, Wilkie often laughed as J limped around campus. He reminded him of their date with destiny and how he was going to "smoke" J in the 40.

Race Day

On the day of the race, J and Wilkie met inside the dome on the University of Northern Iowa campus. All the instructors stopped teaching to witness the event. J got into his stance facing forward; Wilkie got into his backward stance. And at the sound of the whistle, both lunged forward.

Wilkie's start was incredibly fast, even though going backward. He took the early lead, but only for about 10 yards. Robinson caught him. The two were neck and neck for the next 10 yards, then J seemed to channel some cosmic energy and took off like a rocket. Bad knees and all, he blew Wilkie away, easily winning the race.

I didn't think about this event again until this past summer in China. Whilst training outdoors I couldn't help but notice several men and women who were walking and running backward.

This reminded me of a wrestler on the Iowa team, King Mueller (and yes, his name really was 'King' – what's more his brother's name was Reno), who had monstrously muscular calves. One day King was asked by a teammate how he got his calves so big. King replied, "Running uphill… backward."

I can't say for sure whether the backward running of uphill sprints will give you massive calves, but it will give them a sensational workout. Not only that, merely running or walking backward is great exercise for your body and mind. It hits the leg muscles and lower back in ways they have never experienced. In fact, backward training strengthens your kidneys, your heart and brain.

When my son, Frank, was a little over a year old, my wife, Zhannie, saw him walking backward. She immediately said, "In China we say that a child who can walk backward is very smart." How smart? I can't quantify my answer, but I can tell you the more I train in reverse, the sharper my memory and the keener my thinking.

I encourage you to add some backward walking or running into your routine. I also encourage backward sprints. I like to do them at the beach. That way if I fall, I hit a soft surface. All this is covered in depth in my Dao Zou program, which you can read about on my website at **mattfurey.com**.

One of the ideal benefits of running backward sprints is what won't happen to you – or should I say, "shouldn't happen to you?" What could that be? Well, how about the infamous hamstring pull? If you pull a hamstring running a backward sprint, then, as the saying goes, I'll be a monkey's uncle.

21

Upside Down Training

"What we have to learn to do, we learn by doing."

—Aristotle

In the hundreds of Chinese fitness and kung fu books I've purchased in China, there's an exercise you'll see repeated over and over. In Mandarin this exercise is called wan yao – meaning "back bend" or "bridge." You'll find this so-called "wrestler's bridge" in yoga books, military training books, kung fu books, and even general fitness books.

I was an eight-year old grade school wrestler when I learned the bridge. My coach was a man named Donnelly, and while he was coaching a hundred boys one winter evening, he grabbed a microphone to bark instructions.

"Head back. Roll back and forth. Touch your nose to the mat. Go from ear to ear," he explained. Because I was upside down and going backward, I couldn't see what I was doing. And I most certainly couldn't feel where I was going. All I know is I never touched my nose to the mat and no one ever corrected me. In fact, when I was in high school, I never saw anyone on my team touching his nose in the bridge. What's worse, I figured that was the right method after reading a number of wrestling books showing athletes bridging without touching their noses to the mat.

The Proper Way

It wasn't until I was in my mid-30's, spending time with Karl Gotch, an old-time professional wrestler, that I finally learned the proper way to bridge.

At first, my upper back and neck were stiff and inflexible at first, so it took a good four months of daily bridging practice before I was touching my nose to the mat. Then it took another two months to touch it consistently and with ease.

The author does a one-arm bridge in Hainan Island, China.

This was before I recognized that there was a meditative or chi kung aspect to bridging. I found that when I focused on the deep breathing and relaxation aspects, I sped up the progress I sought, even though I wasn't trying to speed up. I also found when I included the deep breathing as an essential part of the bridge, I received physical benefits in terms of flexibility and strength, but also spiritual benefits.

During one workout, after completing three minutes worth of deep breathing mixed with bridging, I stood to begin doing another exercise. I was absolutely euphoric when I got up, in part because I'd only taken eight complete breaths in the three minutes. Just as if I was doing the microcosmic orbit or some other chi kung meditation, I inhaled and held my breath. Then I exhaled and waited a few seconds before inhaling again.

Energy Tune-Up

It's a feat unto itself to do this while your body is upside down and bending backwards is a feat in itself. But I never expected how much it would help me tune into energy at a higher level.

After a couple months of bridging combined with deep breathing my martial arts practice took on a whole new power. I was able to sense an opponent's move much faster than before. I felt his intent much more deeply and I was able to manage and control my own energy output much better.

What's more, I began to become more fluid and creative in how I trained or sparred; a new Universe began to unfold; and I discarded some of the things I had been trained to do for over 30 years.

So much of what we can learn and glean from our practice of martial arts can be stifled if we're unwilling to let go and relax at a higher level. Once we relax and let go we discover a higher level of energy.

Bridging and deep breathing help us find that energy faster. Even when we're upside down and going backward.

22

Be True to Yourself

*"Don't let someone else's opinion of you
become your reality."*

– Les Brown

So you want to drop some pounds, get stronger and more flexible. You want more internal power, more self-discipline, and more time to do what truly matters to you.

I applaud you for having these desires. You can make them become a reality. To do so, however, you must be true to yourself even when others try to interfere with your objectives. To succeed at anything you need to be more than mentally tough; you also need to put up a shield of psychic protection – a shield that deflects those who want to disturb your mind or derail you on the path you've chosen.

You may not realize it, but some people will only feel good if you look bad. Your efforts have proven that within the same 24-hour day, you can do much more than work, watch television, eat three squares, complain and go to bed tired.

After You Win

Remember: People love to congratulate a winner – *after* he wins. But don't expect universal support on your way to victory. You're not likely to get it, and if you feel you need it to succeed, you will never make it.

Sometimes you must stand alone and defy the ideas others have about what you should and should not do. I once heard that Walt Disney didn't believe in moving forward with a project unless nearly everyone was against it. If this is true, it's not far removed from what truly happens when you begin your upward trek.

Yes, you will have people who support you. Those will most likely be your instructors, some fellow students or a couple close friends. Other than that, forget about enlisting everyone's support before you advance. If others are going to support you, it won't be until they see your train moving. Not before.

When I was in high school I made a decision to become a champion wrestler who would go on to compete in college for the legendary Dan Gable at the University of Iowa. Thus, I needed to train every single day – and not just once. Two or three training sessions per day were the keys to moving up the ladder.

Alone With My Dreams

Few supported me as I embarked upon my path. At times I felt like I was all alone, yet I didn't care. Why? Because I trained to achieve a goal, not to win friends.

But when I returned from the state finals my senior year, it was amazing how many people wanted to be my friend. These were the same people who kept telling me I would be a failure.

According to an old saying: "Be who you are and see who stays around." It's another way of saying, "Be true to yourself."

Prior to entering the world shuaijiao kung fu tournament in Beijing, China, in 1997, I was the lone voice thinking I had a chance to win a gold medal. Everyone else said they hoped they didn't get beat too badly by the Chinese fighter in his weight class. I didn't win any friends when I let my fellow teammates know I wasn't going there to lose, to anyone, including the Chinese.

Banish the thought that you must think and do everything the way everyone else does in order to be liked. Banish the notion that you can't train too hard because people might think you odd. Get rid of the idea that others might think you foolish for wanting to excel in whatever you truly love to do.

Seize Your Goal

Go after what you want. And never stop moving toward the goals that truly matter most. You won't have a lot of support in the beginning, but there will always be someone you can count on. Follow the guidance you are given. Believe in what you are taught and apply it with deep faith and enthusiasm.

Most of all, be true to yourself and what you believe. Do this and you will stand out as a rare individual who had the guts and the determination to get the best out of himself, even when others doubted your ability.

23

The Power of a Focused Mind

"All that we are is the result of what we have thought."
– The Buddah

When you read the biographies and autobiographies of famous people, your soul is stirred to greater heights. In 1984, I read a book about the great Chicago Bears running back in the 1960's, Gale Sayers, and it gave me an idea that immediately improved my ability to concentrate on a goal and achieve it.

Sayers often took a seat in an empty football stadium, and while sitting there, he held a football in his hands. He would look at this football for long periods of time, just as a Zen monk would stare at a candle. One time, when someone saw him sitting by himself, he was asked what he was doing. "Concentrating," Sayers said.

After I read this about Sayers and began implementing the practice, I was initially amazed at how good it made me feel. I first used the technique after wrestling practice at the Carver-Hawkeye Arena in Iowa City. Normally when practice ended, I walked to the upper level, opened one of the exit doors and went home. But on this one day in January, something inside of me clicked. I remembered how Sayers did this so I decided to take a seat in the stands and imitate him.

EXPECT TO WIN – HATE TO LOSE

What, No Football?

I didn't have a football to hold. So I used the book I was carrying as my focusing device. I didn't open it. I didn't read a word. All I did was hold it in my hands and look at it as closely as I could. I concentrated on this book until it was the only thing I could think about. Then I concentrated longer until I wasn't thinking about anything at all. My mind went quiet; totally blank.

After a few days of focusing in the empty arena after practice, I decided to add another element into the mix. Instead of looking at the book, I stared at the arena floor, and with open eyes, imagined that I was competing in front of a large crowd.

I Wanted a Varsity Match

Until that point, all of my varsity matches for Iowa were in tournaments and away meets. They were never at home. So while I sat there I imagined that I was wrestling a varsity match before the home crowd. I focused on this image with the same level of concentration that I had previously applied to the book I held.

Four days later, on a Saturday, Iowa was scheduled to wrestle Penn State. The day after we would host Ohio State.

On the date of the Penn State match, the Iowa coaches told me that Penn State brought some reserves along and their coaches wanted to have a couple exhibition matches. Incidentally, in the three years I was at Iowa, this was a first and I wouldn't be surprised if it hasn't happened since.

Anyway, one of the guys Penn State brought along was a 177-pounder. The Iowa coaches asked me to compete against him, even though I was a 167-pounder. I readily agreed, seeing this as my chance to finally wrestle in front of the Iowa crowd. I won the match, 11-3, and loved the sound of the crowd cheering my name.

A Surprising Opportunity

Later that night, when Pete Bush, Iowa's defending national champion at 190-pounds took the mat, he wasn't himself. In the second period, the unthinkable happened. He got pinned.

Afterward the coaches discovered Bush had the flu. They figured he might not be ready for Ohio State the next day, so they pulled me aside and said, "Furey, we may need you tomorrow. Be ready."

At 190 pounds? Two weight classes up.

The next morning I made weight in with my winter clothes still on, including my boots, and I was still underweight. The coaches told me that Bush was still slated to wrestle, but to "play it by ear" as they may change their minds.

When the 158-pound match began, I was given the nod. I would be competing in place of Pete Bush at 190 pounds.

The team score was close so the pressure was on. If I lost we were in danger of losing the match.

Run the Mental Movie

Before taking the mat, I pictured all the moves I knew. I strung them together like a movie and reviewed them in my mind. The very second I walked onto the mat I sensed all would go well.

At the start of the third period I held a commanding 8-3 lead. Fifteen seconds later, I countered my opponent's fireman's carry with a pancake-style hip toss. As soon as he hit the mat, the ref slapped the mat and called him pinned. The crowd went nuts.

Following the match I signed autographs for ten minutes while reporters interviewed me. The television cameras rolled and later that evening, highlights from the match, as well as my post-match interviews were aired throughout the state.

Did the time I spent focusing in the stands have anything to do with what happened that weekend?

Without a doubt.

Both of my matches were not only in front of the Iowa crowd. They were two of the most focused matches of my collegiate career. And they set the stage for a much brighter future.

Not only that, but both matches were at weight classes I didn't compete in. The coaches could have chosen a reserve at 177 or 190 pounds – but they chose me.

Gale Sayers' secret worked.

Park in Front of Your Business

Years later I used this same tool in business. Late at night, when I was finished seeing clients, I'd go for dinner. Afterward I'd pull my car into the parking lot in front of my studio and sit. With my eyes wide open I'd picture new clients coming to me. I'd envision having a full slate. I'd picture more clients coming to me than I could even train.

I have no doubt this paved the way for my first best-seller in fitness, **Combat Conditioning**, as well as the seminars I've held over the years.

Yes, there's tremendous power in a focused, concentrated mind.

24

Be Willing to Move Heaven and Earth

"If you don't know where you are going,
you might wind up someplace else."

— Yogi Berra

I was sitting in a sauna in Beijing, China, during Christmas of 1997, dropping a couple pounds before weigh-ins for the kung fu world championships. As the sweat dripped off my skin I remember thinking that there were three main keys to winning in anything.

* **The first key is clarity of purpose.** Knowing what you want; picturing what you want; and being able to imagine having what you want so deeply that you *feel* as if you already have it.

In my case, it was winning the gold medal. I imagined winning it while I trained; while I ran hill sprints; while I sparred and practiced. I saw the medal around my neck long before tournament time.

When I ran the hills I saw myself on the victory stand with the gold medal hanging around my neck. I pictured the future and enthusiastically told myself, *"I will win the world title this year, in Beijing, at 198 pounds."*

When self-doubt crept in, I strengthened my mental image. I made it bigger and stronger. I brought the image closer to myself. I also raised the intensity and the volume of my message.

The author with Hall of Fame catcher Yogi Berra.

This practice not only made the grueling training bearable, it focused my mind like a laser. Combining physical activity with mental activity is like simultaneously moving heaven and earth. You are pulling the future into the present so you can make the future your reality.

* ***The second key to winning is recognizing you haven't accomplished what you are imagining yet,*** even though you're imagining it as if you have. Regardless, you still have to go out there and go after it.

This is where so many self-development programs error. They tell you to visualize what you want, but they stop short of letting you know there's something you must DO to make what you want a reality.

Testing Your Desire

Using your imagination helps, but it doesn't do the entire job. Your imagination sets the stage for the actors to play their roles, but take the stage they must. And they take the stage through practice, practice and more practice – mental rehearsal as well as physical movement.

Daily practice is how you test your desire. Are you willing to do whatever it takes to meet your goal? Are you willing to move heaven and earth?

Refusal to practice your art or look at where you are in relation to your target is like putting a cast on the muscles of your WILL.

Knowing where your target is, as well as the starting point and mid-points, enhances your mental power. Remember, for a map to work there has to be a Point B (your destination) as well as your Point A (starting point).

* **The third key to winning is the willingness to cooperate with the forces of nature.** You don't simply sit back and expect success to happen. Nor do you work, work, work without sufficient rest or relaxation.

To maximize a plant's growth, you don't water it day and night; nor do you give it nothing but sunshine. Everything has to be in balance. You train and then you let go. You picture what you want, then you let go of the image and feel the future result you desire coming back to the present. You remain open, ready and willing to move heaven and earth to make your goal a reality. You apply physical and mental force, but you do it in a relaxed manner.

These are the keys to success. They worked for me in Beijing in 1997, and they've been working ever since. They are simple, common-sense principles, which over a lifetime, can be continually improved and perfected.

25

Believing is Seeing

"The man who has no imagination has no wings."
– Muhammad Ali

Dr. Wayne Dyer wrote a book in 1989 called, *You'll See it When You Believe It*. I remember seeing him LIVE in San Jose, California, right as the book hit the stores. He spoke for four riveting hours that night.

During an intermission I took my book to him and waited patiently as he signed it. I still have it in my library, along with the notes I penned that night.

Yesterday I saw my old copy on the shelf. I opened it and began re-reading the introduction. I thought back to when I first read this book and began thinking about the importance of continually reviewing what we've learned.

Making Progress

This is how we progress down the path of mastery in martial arts. We study an art form and repeat it until we've supposedly "got it." Then we add to it – perhaps studying other arts or progressing in the same art. Regardless, at least once a year it's important to review the basics; to go back in time and look at the books, courses and materials that helped pave the way.

It's okay to see a trail of dead bodies behind you when you reflect on your career, because these bodies represent the body of the old you. But YOU they aren't. They're simply memories of who you thought you were "before."

Setting Your Goals

It may seem strange but the ONE person weaving his way through all your memories is the intangible spirit of YOU that cannot be touched. This is the YOU who set goals and practiced.

This YOU can be experienced in the theater of your mind. In your imagination you can think anything you want, and be anything you want. You can learn two skills, or 15. You can practice slow or like thunder and lightning; and you can exhibit grace or power.

Here's all you need to make what you're picturing a reality:

1. Picture what you want on a regular basis.
2. Add desire (feeling) to the picture through deep breathing.
3. Command your mind to accomplish what you want.
4. Move your body – take action.
5. Allow yourself to become what you want by believing you deserve it.

Form a Mental Picture

When you want to make a change in anything about yourself, form a mental picture of what you want.

But this alone isn't enough. If it were, then everything you've ever pictured, even one time, for one second, would have manifested in your reality.

You need to add feeling to the mental picture through deep breathing and concentration to cause a shake-up in your reality. You've got to add desire. And you've got to put in time everyday to develop the level of skill you have in mind.

SEE what you want long before you get there. When you see what you want and have the desire to get there, it's only natural that you believe you can get it. You don't believe because you see. You see because you believe. Or as Wayne Dyer wrote, "You'll see it when you believe it."

The author practicing the art of mental imagery.

26

Burn the Past

*"I skate to where the puck is going to be,
not to where it has been."*

– Wayne Gretzky

Sometimes a master teacher plants a seed inside of us and it takes years before the bud grows large enough to be understood.

My initial experience with this came from Dan Gable, my first college wrestling coach. It was 1982, during my freshman year in college and we had won yet another national championship. And it was time for the annual victory pig roast.

The party began at noon and ran until early the next morning. That year, during the dark of night, a few minutes before midnight, when I was standing before the fireplace with a number of others, Coach Gable approached and handed me a newspaper article about himself.

He asked me to read it aloud. As I read the clipping I learned of a victory Gable had achieved many years earlier. I could feel the positive chills it gave everyone who listened to the account.

And when I finished reading, Gable did something I did not expect: He took the clipping from me and put it into the fire.

I stood paralyzed, unable to speak. The man I so greatly admired was taking remnants from his past, reliving them once again, then burning them before my eyes.

A Turning Point

At the time, I didn't realize the spiritual implications of Gable's actions. I wasn't a champion at the level he was and the last thing I would ever do was burn positive press about myself. Yet, my talent was still green and undeveloped, and so I was, in a sense, clinging to "who I was" as a wrestler instead of releasing the past to become someone better.

I cannot say what was going through Gable's mind when this westernized version of an Indian puja took place. But two important lessons sprouted through the soil when I recalled this event:

First, whenever we want to attract something of a higher nature into our lives, we may need to detach from what we have. This is referred to as the "Law of Vacuum." Essentially, if we want to become stronger, we need to give up weakness. If we want to become a more highly skilled martial artist, we need to give up laziness and lack of focus. We need to look at ourselves objectively and see what we are creating. In short, if we want to make room for more, we empty ourselves.

By giving up the clipping from the past, Gable was saying to the Universe, "I am not identified with my victories. I use the memories of them to grow, but I'm letting this one go in order to bring another one to me at a higher level."

Burn the Negative

Secondly, many of us carry the past with us in a self-defeating way. We'd be well-advised to burn the negative that no longer serves us and remember the positive experiences.

If Gable was willing to detach from a victorious clipping about himself, then we can most assuredly learn to detach and rise above all our mistakes, failures and setbacks. We can offer them up. We can give them up. We can rid ourselves of the negative and find something better.

Take a few moments to think about something you'd like to bring into your life. Now think of something you can give up from the past to make space for it. Have a little midnight ceremony for yourself. Light a fire and burn the past. I think you'll be amazed at what this practice will bring into your life.

The author sprints up a hill of sand in the Gobi Desert.

27

Counting Leads to Success

"What gets measured gets done, what gets measured and fed back gets done well, what gets rewarded gets repeated."

– John E. Jones

I was recently in Ningxia province, in western China, visiting several historical sites, running up mountains of sand in the desert and riding camels. T'was well over 100 degrees in the shade by mid-morning, so I made sure to do my exercises early.

As I loosened up I couldn't help but notice one man practicing his kung fu forms with a long mop, the kind with braided strands of rope. What a great idea, I thought. Getting whipped across the face with a mop could blind you and leave you with a dozen or more lacerations. If you take away everyone's guns, you've still got a few make-shift weapons if you look around the house.

Training Day

Later that day, I saw another man training in the parking lot several stories below my hotel window. We was walking backward the breadth and length of a square. I watched for a few minutes, then took the elevator down to see if he'd answer a few questions.

"I noticed you walking backward," I said. "This is something I like to practice as well. May I ask, how long do you walk backward?"

"I walk backward for 2,000 steps," he explained. "Two-thousand is the minimum number I do. And I make sure I don't finish in less than 30 minutes."

We talked about the benefits of training backward: less pounding on the joints; improved posture and greater cardiovascular output.

My Chinese friend, Fan, who goes with me everywhere, then told the man I was a former world champion in shuaijiao kung fu. He seemed surprised, so I demonstrated a few forms. He smiled and nodded, then told how he practices tai chi every morning and does an array of spinning exercises. He put his arms in the air at shoulder-height and began to spin counter-clockwise a dozen times.

"I've been doing this exercise for three years now," he said.

"How many do you do each day?" I asked.

"Thirty-six," he replied.

Mental Notes

Although I didn't have a pad and paper, I was taking mental notes at warp speed. Every time he mentioned an exercise, he stressed how he counted the steps and repetitions.

This made me think of the saying, "Everything in life is math."

Whether or not you agree, I have compared the skills of those who do and do not keep score in whatever they do. And I've found that those who count are utilizing a powerful self-improvement tool. It helps them succeed faster, even when they don't realize it. On the other foot, those who refuse to count usually don't improve much.

Those who count are much more focused than those who don't. It's like having a deadline for a goal or project versus not having one.

When we have a deadline, we know it will get done. When the date is open, there will always be a major dose of procrastination around.

I am amazed when I observe people who don't count their repetitions when they train. You see someone skipping rope. You ask him how many reps he's done and he has no clue. He might as well be sleeping. He's most certainly not aware, awake or fully conscious as he trains.

Make it Count

When I train, every exercise I do is consciously counted. If I'm doing pushups, I count every rep. I set a goal before I start. I declare how many I want to do, then I begin training and I count until my results match my intentions.

Without counting, the mind tends to be scattered and unfocused. When we count, immediate order comes into our lives. Counting is a form of meditation. Know your numbers. Pay attention to what you're doing from the first to the last number. When you know your numbers, you can improve them. When you're in the dark about them, you'll remain in the dark, unable to improve or reach a goal.

Want motivation? Then drop to the floor right now and see how many sit-ups and/or pushups you can do. Count the reps. Write them down along with the date. Then set a goal for how many you'd really like to do. Each day do the exercise again and record the result. Do this and you'll soon hit a minimum number you'll feel compelled to do each day.

Like the man doing at least 2,000 backward steps each workout, you'll also find your magic number. And each day you hit or exceed this number, it will go down in history as a *power day*, a day in which you connected your mind and body to create a desired result.

28

Do The Thing You Fear

*"He who is not everyday conquering some fear
has not learned the secret of life."*

– Ralph Waldo Emerson

Everyone knows the meaning of fear. Maybe it's fear of death; fear of poverty; fear of old age or fear of failure; or success; or that old dandy: fear of criticism.

Whatever the fear, rest assured that in most cases, the fear is unwarranted. It's also holding you back from living your dreams.

Successful living isn't so much "lack of fear" as it is MASTERY of fear. And most people in martial arts will tell you they began their training to conquer some sort of fear. Funny thing is, there are levels upon levels of fear. Literally. And when you conquer one level you'll meet another if you continue to challenge yourself. Conquer it and along comes another. When you're done what you've feared, you literally kill the fear – you put it to death.

Don't Fear Fear

Then again, you only killed the fear you had in that specific arena. Place yourself in another arena and perhaps the whole ball game begins again.

For example, at one time I was afraid of flying. To conquer my fear, I kept hopping a plane to go somewhere. I recognized that the key to conquering my fear of flying was to do what I feared. Yes, it would have been easier to stay home, but that was not the right way. I would conquer my fear of flying by getting on a plane and adjusting my mental state to what was going on inside the plane, outside the plane and most importantly, inside my mind.

When turbulence hit, my perfect emotional state would get rattled. Oh, another area for me to conquer. And conquer it I did. Over and over again. Today, when the wind blows the plane around, it's just wind. It's not that awful turbulence.

This is the approach to take when conquering fear in any endeavor. You catch that little fear monger creeping up behind you, or popping up on your shoulder, but instead of being its victim, you slap it down and sweep it away.

When I was competing, there were moments, just before a match, when I experienced fear. Not fear of my opponent, but rather, the fear of fatigue or the fear of being humiliated when you're fatigued. The two often go hand-in-hand. I overcame this fear by making conditioning my ultimate weapon, and by doing deep breathing exercises or chi kung before competition. Focusing on my breathing and visualizing being above the fear would help me enter the arena without a worry in the world.

Dominating Fear

All great martial artists recognize when fear approaches. Once you're conscious of a fear, you have the ability to choose whether you're going to let the fear dominate and control you, or if you're going to rule and dominate it.

Champions don't let it rule them. They see the fear. They feel the fear. And they proceed anyway.

Ralph Waldo Emerson once said, "Do the thing you fear and the death of fear is certain."

How true.

To master fear and "do the thing," it helps if you understand how to relax, breathe deeply and flip your mental switch to a positive channel. All of us have the capacity to "flip the switch." This not only helps us change the mental image that is bothering us, but it also changes the corresponding feeling that goes with the image.

I knew a guy who was afraid of snakes – so much so that when he went for a walk he would worry about a snake attacking him. One day he decided to flip the switch. Whenever an image of a snake attacking him came to mind, he changed it to an image of himself walking triumphantly through water on the beach. The new image obliterated the fear.

These examples are proof that you can master anything you fear, as long as you remember to do the thing you fear. Thus, you gain power and mastery over your life that cannot be attained sitting on the couch. If you're hoping that your fear will go away on its own without you confronting it, think again. Do the thing you fear and the death of fear is certain.

29

Don't Make It Harder
Than It Is

"Make everything as simple as possible, but not simpler."
— Albert Einstein

When you begin martial arts training you learn to relax, breathe and focus. You learn when to use force and when to absorb another's energy. This comes with an understanding that you can make anything in life easier or tougher than it really is.

For example, whenever you make a mistake you have many options on how to respond. You can get upset at yourself and try harder. Yet, in trying harder you may be putting the wrong type of energy into your training and it can make you worse. You might be stiffening your muscles, holding your breath or tensing your face, which in the end are impeding your task.

Wrong Direction

Whenever your body is not working in harmony with your mind, an inner alarm needs to go off; an alarm that helps you realize part of your extra effort is leading in the wrong direction.

I believe an alarm does go off – and often – but without even realizing it many people have trained themselves to ignore the alarms.

When winning and losing or life and death are on the line, you might think there's no time to adjust yourself mentally. But if you train the way you'll compete, your reactions are calm and cool regardless of the situation.

How you breathe and focus becomes even more important when you're in pain. I've suffered a number of injuries and can tell you that I never benefited by grimacing or stifling my breath. I won a national title in wrestling with a painful rib injury that got re-injured during every practice over a two-month period. I endured the pain, but there was an easier way. I just didn't know it at the time. Today the left side of my lower ribcage bears no resemblance to the right side.

Dig Deeper

Sometimes in the heat of battle you must call upon every ounce of physical and mental strength. When you have nothing left you need to dig deeper and pull something from the spiritual. Once you've summoned this extra energy, use it to propel yourself forward.

If you've never experienced this, you may wonder how a martial artist or athlete finds his second-wind, or summons a spiritual power. What does he look like? How is he breathing? What is he picturing in his mind and saying to himself to get such spectacular results?

I can tell you that once you've exhausted everything you have, your body has no choice other than relaxation. And when your body is relaxed, your breathing is deep and full. At this point, if you want to summon further resources, form a mental picture of yourself rising above the fray and surging to victory.

Many athletes go through each and every practice in the "I can't do it" mode. They feel stress and tension in everything they do. The reason can be found in the way they form pictures in their minds and how they talk to themselves.

When most people attempt a difficult task, they believe it will take a lot of hard work to become proficient. Yet, when a baby learns to walk, was that considered hard work? What about learning to talk? Was it hard for a baby to learn a foreign language?

Relaxed Training

No, it was relaxed training. The baby is a super learner and the perfect model for how adults can quickly improve their results if they'll breathe deeply and relax their muscles.

Don't just use your mind to go beyond the so-called limits of your body. Use your breathing, your structure and every muscle of your body. Train with a sense of wonder and it will help you enter the realm of effortless power.

This sense of effortless power eventually becomes the norm. All your hard training leads to being relaxed and at ease while doing what used to be hard. Your power is relaxed because you're not making it harder than it is.

30

Get Out of Town

*"The world is a book and those who do not travel
read only one page."*

— St. Augustine

Years ago, when I was living in California, I was often shocked to discover how many residents had never left the state. I understand this to some extent since California is enormous when compared to Rhode Island. In California alone you have mountains, the ocean, the desert and farmlands. There's plenty of variety to keep you excited.

At the same time, I don't understand it, especially amongst fellow martial artists. How can you study kung fu or tai chi and never even consider visiting China? Martial artists who don't set a goal to travel to other countries to learn, never really get their mind cracked open, nor do they encounter the suspense or the emotional flexibility needed to get along in virtually any situation.

Traveling With Your Mind?

There are those who would argue with me. They will say that you can travel just as much, if not more, within your own mind as you do throughout the world.

And I agree. You can. Yet, most great masters traveled to learn their art and later on traveled again to begin teaching it. Think about it:

The author visits the Shaolin Temple.

What would martial arts be today in the United States without masters who came here from abroad, as well as Americans who traveled overseas to learn.

Those who don't travel often lack broad experience, have a limited way of thinking about the world, and find it much more difficult to explore within, simply because they haven't seen enough to be challenged as a person.

There's a scene in Star Wars when Luke Skywalker is training with Yoda in a remote, swampy area. The young, inexperienced Skywalker tells Yoda that he is not afraid, to which Yoda grimaces and whispers in a raspy voice, "YOU WILL BE!"

Get Challenged

This is the truth about traveling to countries wherein you don't know the language and are unfamiliar with the idiosyncrasies of the culture. You may feel brave and courageous sitting at home, but you're hardly being challenged. In a foreign country wherein English is not spoken and everything is new, your buttons will get pushed at a whole new level. Once you get to a point where you remain calm in the midst of chaos, then you've made progress, both psychological and spiritual.

On a different scale, similar progress can be made when you attend a seminar that challenges you to the core. You need challenges to your skills, knowledge and the beliefs you have about yourself.

Sure, you can stay at home and think you already have everything within you that you'll ever need to succeed.

But try to think of a single person of substance who failed to get out of the familiar scene he was comfortable in. History's great people either traveled by choice or by force.

"All things considered," wrote Rudyard Kipling, "there are only two kinds of men in this world – those who stay home and those who do not. The second are the more interesting." St. Augustine once wrote, "The world is a book and those who do not travel read only one page."

I recently visited Bodhidharma's cave on Song Mountain near the Shaolin Temple in China. The power emanating from this sacred spot was truly incredible. After entering the cave and experiencing the energy, I hiked to the top of the mountain and sat at the base of the giant Bodhidharma statue. I got a view of life that few will ever experience, because they never plan to go elsewhere. They tell themselves they cannot afford it and never consider that they could if they set a goal to make it happen.

I couldn't afford it either when I began traveling. I made a decision to get up and go and the funds needed to make the trip showed up in my life. That's how it works. You decide to become a person with certain skills before you have the skills, and then you get them. You decide to travel before you have the money, and then the money comes. The key factor is DECIDING upon what you want.

What decision are you going to make today about your future? Make a different one right now and I guarantee your life will change. Be brave. Be courageous. Get out of town.

31

Gold Medal Clues

*"You can't put a limit on anything. The more you
dream, the farther you get."*

– Michael Phelps

Watching Michael Phelps' sensational and surreal come-from-behind finish in the finals of the 100-meter butterfly (in the Beijing 2008 Olympics) was living proof of why you never want to count yourself out. Phelps was in seventh place at the end of 50 meters – seventh among eight.

As I watched I told my son, "He's going to get the bronze. Wait, maybe the silver. Wait, oh my goodness, he may pull this one out. Aaaah – oh my God – he just won. HE WON!!!"

Wow.

Leading the race was Milorad Cavic, who let up at the finish. Cavic glided in for the touch while Phelps hustled to get one more powerful stroke. Phelps' decision to never give up was the difference between gold and silver.

Think of this. How often do we glide to the finish in our lives when one final burst would do us much more good? How often do we perform our routine with a "ho-hum" attitude? How often do we count ourselves out because we're not in the lead when we begin? How often do we think "It cannot be done" simply because the road looks difficult?

Banish these thoughts and GO FOR IT. Put all the force from your entire being into your endeavors. Remember your intention. What are you trying to accomplish? And why? Recall the what and the why before every practice and you'll be catapulted forward with a gold medal surge.

When you focus on and add energy to your intention, you may not come in first or win the gold every time, but you will have given everything you have in pursuit of what you want, and that is the most you can realistically ever ask of yourself.

Yet, so few people give their all to anything. Ever. They're half-committed. And half-committed doesn't work.

The key to success is being totally committed to your goal.

Seal your links in your mind and in your body as you practice. Observe where your intention feels weak. Note where you're vulnerable. Strengthen those areas. Leave no escape route from what you said you would do.

"I Dare and I Do"

Focus on what you want and go after it with everything you have. If you feel your intention beginning to weaken, then repeat to yourself, "I CAN AND I WILL. I DARE AND I DO." Say this out loud in a commanding voice. Whisper it as well. See yourself where you want to be. See yourself moving forward, reaching your goal and celebrating its achievement.

When you have a goal programmed into your mind; a goal you think about each day; a goal you fertilize with the energy of your own breath; you have a goal that will be brought into reality.

Michael Phelps understands the importance of practicing and competing with gusto, even when it may look like all is lost. And who among us doesn't need a reminder about that? Phelps' gold medal clues are more valuable than his gold medal.

32

How to Get Good Faster

"Be quick but never in a hurry."

– John Wooden

I was in Japan riding the Shinkansen (bullet train) from Tokyo to Kyoto. It moved at a speed of over 300 km per hour, and strangely enough, this high speed is accomplished via magnetic force. You might think 300 km per hour is fast, but another bullet train in Japan has already set a record for traveling at 581 km per hour.

At that speed you might as well be flying – and in a sense you are, because the latest bullet trains are powered by magnetic levitation. By using electro-magnets the bullet trains can literally hover above the train tracks. This means there is no friction between the train and the track.

What's this have to do with your training? As you're cruising in this train, you're totally relaxed and calm. You are neither stressed out nor telling yourself or the train to go faster. You simply allow it to happen.

Be Quick, But Don't Hurry

Today we live in a society in which we're encouraged to move faster and faster, and when we train we think of getting results faster. And there's nothing wrong with this, provided you never lose sight that training is a relaxed journey, even when you're sprinting. You will always improve fastest by training hard with a calm spirit.

When most people give themselves the "faster, faster" command, they tend to stop relaxing. They don't move around as if they're being pulled by a magnetic force. Instead, they act as if it's our body that must do all the work. Not so.

First, feed the mind instructions. That's how you give your internal bullet train a destination. Where are you going and what do you want when you get there?

When you have the answers, start moving but stay relaxed. This means you don't tense your face or flex your back. Doing that forces the rest of your body to become tense, and you'll feel rundown instead of uplifted. And while you're tearing yourself down with the "faster, faster" mantra, you get nowhere.

Barking at yourself and tensing your muscles is not the best way to improve your skills. The fact is, the method I have just described slows you down more than you'd like to know. A faster way to get things done is accomplished by relaxing, breathing deeply, focusing on exactly what it is that you want, then allowing your energy to be pulled in the direction of the objective you want until you've accomplished it.

Quick, But Relaxed

Again, think of the bullet train. It's moving at blazing speeds, yet it is relaxed and so are all the passengers. The job is getting done quicker than ever, yet no one is stressed out about it. This is the image you want to keep in mind as you train.

See yourself zooming toward what you want. As you zoom, stay relaxed, centered and calm. Don't let a frown occupy space in your mind or on your face. If you feel your neck and shoulders raise, tell them to relax and feel them drop to a natural resting position.

Breathe deeply as you move. See yourself at the end of the line – at your predetermined destination. See yourself getting where you want to go without friction or resistance.

Relax and let your energy flow. Remove the resistance from your mind and body. Let the magnets pull you along the tracks. Keep these images in mind and you can achieve whatever you want with far less effort. You'll know the secret of how to get good faster.

The author practicing kung fu in Switzerland.

33

How Strong is Your Desire?

"Burning desire to be or do something gives us staying power — a reason to get up every morning or to pick ourselves up and start in again after a disappointment."

— Marsha Sinetar

When I was a high school wrestler, I remember the day I was heart-broken after I lost a match. I went to workout the next day and Tom, a former college wrestler, asked me how I did. When I told him I lost, he looked at me and said, "It all boils down to DESIRE."

His comment stung. I thought I was working hard. I thought I was putting in enough time to win, but he wasn't talking about that. He wasn't talking about my work ethic or how much sweat I put into my practice.

He was talking about an internal quality: DESIRE.

When I was a freshman in college, I thought I was busting my hump in practice each day. Then one day, some eight months into my first year, I got another wake up call on the same topic.

I was sitting in the Jacuzzi with my coach, Dan Gable, silently kneading my aching muscles. After about five minutes of silence, Gable looked at me and said, "You know Furey, I've noticed that you don't really try very hard in practice. When I put a kindergarten half-nelson on you, you just roll over and get pinned."

When Gable said this to me I felt like a loser. But something clicked. I didn't realize I had a lot more inside until I heard these words. I thought I was trying hard, but I wasn't. I needed more DESIRE. Gable helped me realize this. To this day I believe if he never took the time to tell me I wasn't trying hard enough, I might not have ever figured it out on my own.

I changed after Gable told me what I didn't necessarily want to hear. I was determined to do better, to show him I could fight harder.

Twice as Good

Next day in the practice room, I was twice as good as before. I executed the same moves I already knew, but now I did them with snap and ginger. Yet, the only change I made was "internal." I simply decided to give more than I had previously given, to wrestle with more desire. A year later a fellow teammate told me he overheard Gable telling others on the team that I was the most improved wrestler in the room. I still wasn't a champion. I still had a long way to go. But by strengthening my desire to succeed, I improved dramatically.

A couple years later, after I'd won a few major tournaments, including an NCAA II championship, I realized that part of my mission in life was to help others strengthen their desire to succeed.

I came to this realization when my collegiate career ended and I was uncertain of my future. Then I received a letter from a young high school wrestler in Alaska. He had attended a wrestling camp in Oregon where I was a coach, and he was upset because he was a senior and was having a terrible season. When he wrote to me his record was 2-4. I remembered the boy from the camp so I wrote him back. In my letter I told him that success in wrestling, and any other endeavor, boiled down to one word: DESIRE.

The person who WANTS it most is usually the one who wins.

I told him to write his goal on a card, read it aloud every morning and night, and to focus on it as often as possible throughout the day.

Three weeks later I received a surprise phone call from the boy. He announced himself by saying, "You're talking to a state champion from Alaska." The boy told me he did exactly as I had told him to do, and it turned around his career.

Going Through The Motions

What I have just told you is basic and fundamental to the achievement of any goal you have in life. Yet, where do most people err? In the basics and fundamentals. They go through the motions of training. Yet, the desire is not there. The focus is half-cooked. And as a result, you don't do as well as you'd like.

Unfortunately, strengthening your desire is not something you do once and then you're set for life. That's the lesson I had to learn after my senior year in college. I won titles when my desire was strongest. I lost when it was much weaker.

Sure, you can work hard and have success elude you. But once you set your mind and heart on a target, once you feel the vibration of success pulsating within you, you are on the way to achieving something spectacular.

Success will elude you UNTIL you learn to train your physical muscles and your internal muscles we call "mind." You also train the internal skills that transform ordinary individuals into extraordinary creators.

And ramping up your DESIRE is an internal skill.

Even if you visualize what you want and work toward the attainment of it, you can be lacking in desire. If you have to compete against others who have far more desire than you do, this challenges you to give more, do more and experience success at higher levels.

Make no mistake: If your desire is weak, you'll have trouble getting what you want. Your desire must be strong if you want a shift to take place. And once this shift takes place inside, rest assured it is taking place outside of you as well.

Once your desire is pulsating, you'll find that the goal you seek is also seeking you. And so the question: How strong is your desire to succeed right now?

Aaah, come on, you can do better than that!

The author practicing at the beach in St. Petersburg, Florida.

34

How to Stop Losing and Start Winning

"Our greatest glory is not in never falling,
but in rising every time we fall."

– Confucius

In his book **Iron and Silk**, Mark Salzman tells the story of Master Liang, a tai chi push hands champion from Hunan province in China. In his youth, Liang was also a champion weightlifter, but despite his tremendous strength, he was easily defeated when pushing hands. In fact, during his first five years of practice, he lost every bout he entered.

How did this strong man, who couldn't win in push hands, eventually become a champion? The answer has as much to do with the way you THINK, as well as how you keep track of what does and does not work.

Formula for Success

What was Master Liang's success formula? First, each day he would go to the park and practice with the best push hands people he could find.

Secondly, after he lost, he would go home and record every mistake he made in a little notebook. He would then spend time thinking about what he could do to correct his mistakes. Instead of seeing his mistakies as bad, he saw them as the feedback that would help guide him to the top.

Bear in mind that Master Liang did this for five years before he turned the tide in his favor; before he won a single bout. If true, this observation alone is worth its weight in platinum. It shows Liang's internal strength and character; it shows his persistence, determination and desire–qualities grossly lacking in so many people today.

After five years of tracking his efforts, Liang started to win a few matches. This leads to step three in his success formula.

When Master Liang began to win, he recorded what he did correctly. He recorded the how and the why concerning his victories. And he continued to take notes this way until he won every time he pushed hands with someone.

Record of Achievement

The key point is that Liang recorded the details of his matches for many, many years. This showed his willingness to do FAR more than anyone else. It also showed how he was willing to go through the physical as well as mental parts of his training. He kept track of the how and why of his successes and failures. He took time to analyze his mistakes until he figured out how to correct them.

The person who acknowledges his mistakes and looks for ways to correct them is way ahead of the pack. His mental focus and his vision penetrates deep beneath the surface of reality. If you're willing to follow Liang, you will be like the boxer who gets up every time he is knocked down. Those who continue to rise after each fall never taste defeat. They use their defeats as a springboard to success. They use their mistakes and the feedback from them to stop losing and start winning.

35

I Dare You to Succeed

*"The principle is competing against yourself.
It's about self-improvement, about being better
than you were the day before."*

— Steve Young

How often do you hear about people being dared to do something great? How often has anyone ever dared you to make the most of yourself – to break through barriers and reach new heights?

If it weren't for great teachers, most of us would never challenge ourselves to become more than we are. Yet, even when you have a great teacher, you're still the one who makes the decision to succeed. You're still the one who accepts the dare.

Last night I was out bowling with a group of people from my son's class. One of the people in the group, Bob, saw that I was ahead of him. He didn't say anything at first, but I sensed he was not taking his weak performance in a professional manner.

Visualize the Result

Regardless of how I was doing, before hurling each ball I stepped up to the line, breathed deeply and got mentally ready. I visualized the result I wanted before I tossed the ball and this must have bothered Bob because when he saw me concentrating, he said: "Come on, Matt. Throw a gutter ball. We need a gutter ball."

"You must be talking to the 'little floor mat' that is sitting right here on the floor," I said to him with a quick sideward glance. "You can't be talking to ME."

He smiled in a way that let everyone know he'd been caught. He closed his mouth and stared in the opposite direction as I looked straight ahead and refocused on throwing a perfect strike.

Daring Me to Fail

The man was daring me to throw a gutter ball just the same as some people are daring you to fail; daring you to not give life your best. He was hoping I'd be unable to nullify his negativity. He was daring me to be less than I'm capable of so he could feel better about performing at such a low level.

I blocked his comments outwardly and internally. And as I stepped up to the line I kept the mental picture of what I wanted: a strike.And whammo, I got one.

Biggest Opponent

Years ago I was getting ready to spar with a man who loved to talk tough. He openly proclaimed that he was going to put a whooping on me. I smiled and said, "We'll see."

He continued talking tough, apparently not getting the message. I kept my focus and when we finally squared off he took a beating.

The greatest achievers compete with themselves more than against others and that's how they become great. They dare themselves to conquer one obstacle after another, including what others say and do around them. No matter what, they keep their focus.

Those who think success is dependent on your opponent being helpful, courteous and friendly don't understand the art of the dare.

Anyone can dare you to be stupid. It's up to you to dare yourself to become great.

The author poses before Matt Furey Hope School in Hainan Island, China.

36

The Secret Power of 'S'

"It's what you learn after you know it all that counts."

— John Wooden

Albert Einstein said that asking questions is the key to acquiring knowledge. I have found this to be true. Whatever you want to learn can be learned by asking questions, provided you're patient enough to wait for an answer and wise enough to ferret out the good answers from the bad.

We can turn to infinite sources of information when we have questions about how we can improve our skills. These include: our teachers, books, DVDs, CDs, camps and clinics. But what about being open to answers that come from the "ethers" – or those outside our normal means of receiving information?

Waiting for an Answer

Provided you're open-minded, you will undoubtedly flash upon something that will answer a question you've had. At other times, however, you may find your questions being answered in the strangest of places. Sometimes the answers to your questions will come in stages, over a long period of time.

For example, back in 1992, when I was reading a tai chi magazine, I was perplexed by something an author wrote. He said that the most effective techniques in tai chi were those that attacked your opponent in the form of the letter "S." He said circular, coiling, twisting movements were always superior to moves that were directed straight into an opponent's strength.

This made sense to me. I knew from experience that the techniques I performed with a circular movement were difficult to defend against. But I was left with a burning question: What other circular techniques could I come up with? It seemed that most of the attacks I knew were direct attacks, going straight into an opponent's strength, or pounding on him until I found a weakness.

Keep Searching

As I studied kung fu and tai chi, I learned many different ways to move my arms, trunk and body in an S-like manner. These movements helped make my techniques harder to interpret and thus, more difficult to counter. But there had to be more. I kept searching for an answer.

Then one day, I hiked to the bottom of the Grand Canyon with my wife. I wasn't thinking about how I could improve my skills when I went on this hike, but remember what I said: Answers can come to you anytime and anywhere, in the strangest of places.

Well, on our hike back up the canyon, when we were taking a rest to gaze at the wonderful scenery, I looked up at the trail ahead of us – then I looked at the winding trails we had already passed. I noticed how the trails moved in a slightly circular fashion for a few hundred feet, then turned in a half-circle. After a few hundred more feet the trail took another half-circle turn, and so on.

When I looked at the structure of the trails, I asked myself: How successful would I be in hiking this canyon if I walked to the edge of it, stepped off and tried to walk straight down?

Be Open

What does this have to do with success? Everything, if you are open to receiving answers.

The Grand Canyon is a massive natural structure, yet someone figured out how to conquer it on foot. All those S-like movements, (called switch backs in hiker-speak) were the only possible way to successfully go from the top of the canyon to the bottom and back again. Someone looked at this incredible "wonder of the world" and calculated where it was insurmountable, then deduced where it was vulnerable. Someone figured out how circular motions winding through the rocks and trees would lead to a successful journey.

As I looked at these winding trails, my question was being answered in more depth than I could find in any book. I was witnessing nature at its finest – being conquered. I instantly saw how I could improve my skills by adding more of an S-like movement to the basic techniques I had been taught.

I realized I didn't have to invent new moves; I merely had to add a little coiling action to the moves I already knew. The coiling could be in the form of an 'S' or in the form of a 'C.'

After returning home from the Grand Canyon, I eagerly began drilling with one of my students. Moves that I had been showing him for the past two years took on a whole new power. Every time I performed a technique on him, I thought of those winding trails, and I made sure I circled, coiled and moved away from his power, even if I knew I could plow through him if I wanted.

When he grabbed me, instead of resisting his grab, I moved my limbs and waist in a semi-circle. And every time without exception, he lost the power he thought he held over me.

Since that day at the Grand Canyon, in other activities I am involved in, I find myself remembering to coil my body. In the sport of baseball, for example, you'll often see the great hitters turning their feet inward and coiling their inner thighs. You can also take note of how great pitchers have great arm pronation when throwing. And if we really want to talk about the power of the 'S' with pitchers, think of how hard it is to hit a fastball that moves as it enters the strike zone. Or a slider, sinker, curve or cutter. All of these deceptive pitches are designed to take away the hitter's biggest asset without overpowering him.

The Right Questions

Ask yourself the right questions and the answers will come. The answers may evolve over time, they may come gradually, and they may come in the strangest of places or at the strangest times. They might even come from strange sources that you may want to disqualify.

Every time you train you will undoubtedly flash upon ideas that will answer your questions, but these hunches will only come to you if you are open-minded.

Ask yourself what you can do to put a little more of the letters 'S' and 'C' into your existing techniques. Then act upon the answers you receive. Doing so will make a believer out of you.

37

Your Hidden Strength

*"I always felt that my greatest asset was not my physical
ability, it was my mental ability."*

– Bruce Jenner

When I used to wrestle in practice with Olympic gold medalist
and Olympic coach Dan Gable at Iowa, he would put his arms on me
and although he was much lighter, I couldn't budge his arms. Yet,
if Gable and I compared our strength levels in the weight room, I'm
positive I would have outperformed him.

For years I wondered what made Gable feel so much stronger
on the mat? I thought about this a lot when I was at the University of
Iowa. I asked different team members what they thought and their
answers varied quite a bit. Some told me it was because of the position
or angle of his arms. Others told me it was because his body was
relaxed. A few told me it was because he had special tendon strength
that gave him leverage. Another person told me it was because his mind
was so strong.

Gable's Secret

The best answer came to me one day when I was sitting in
the wrestling office at the university watching a videotape of freestyle
matches filmed in Tblisi, Georgia, when it was still part of the former
Soviet Union.

Gable walked in when I was watching one of these matches. A Russian wrestler who was leading an American 8-0 was cautioned for passivity and put in the down position. The American wrapped his arms around the Soviet's chest and tried to turn him. The Soviet flattened out, spread his arms wide and relaxed completely. He almost looked like he was sleeping.

As the two of us watched the action, Gable chuckled a bit and said, "There's no way that Russian is going to get turned. Trying to turn him is like trying to turn the whole mat."

It took me years to fully understand what Gable meant, and ironically, I found my answer studying Chinese martial arts. Based upon what I now know, the Soviet couldn't be turned because he focused his mind and sunk his energy into the earth. This made him feel much heavier than he was. He may have also imagined that his arms and legs extended to each corner of the mat. In his imagination, he was larger than his physical body and this gave him a hidden source of power and strength.

1983-84 National Champion Iowa Wrestling Team –
the author in Row 3 – second from the left.

Larger Than Life

Gable gave me the answer to what he was doing to me when I felt like I couldn't budge him. Gable may have only weighed 155 pounds, but he was LARGER THAN LIFE. He may have only been 5-foot-9, but in his own mind he was a GIANT.

His arms and legs may have been smaller in circumference than mine, but in his imagination they were enormous. And although I may have been stronger in the weight room, the mat room was a different reality. It was a place where human body contact felt like something more. This was especially true when you were working out with someone who knew how to transcend the physical; with someone who knew how to "be the mat" – to make himself more than he appeared to be.

Think of how this concept of imagining yourself "larger than life" applies to anything you do. You don't have to be a wrestler or martial artist to transcend the physical. Every time you imagine yourself being big enough to handle any situation, you are tapping into your hidden strength. There's an inexhaustible supply of this strength at your beck and call. Use it to make yourself invincible.

38

Keep Climbing

*"Nobody's a natural. You work hard to get good and
then work to get better. It's hard to stay on top."*

– Paul Coffey

Practice is just as important as competition. Losses are as crucial to our development as victories. Mistakes lead to success. And life can still be exhilarating after you've climbed the highest mountain in the world.

We can become much better than we realize. Our performance can go way beyond the goals we have, even those we set to win championships or move up in rank. If our training life is only about achieving goals, and winning is the only thing that truly counts, then all the days spent practicing and preparing are simply wasted moments. The journey of our career is overlooked. It is only the destination that matters. This, my friends, is not the best approach. If our sole preoccupation is that of achieving goals, we are bound to become frustrated. Goals are important. But so is living in the present.

Living in the Present

Master Pan is 75-years old and a long-time tai chi player. His form is better now than it has ever been. He has practiced tai chi everyday for over 50 years, and the physical and *mental* skills he has today are superior to those of his youth.

This demonstrates that the commonly held notion of skills deteriorating simply because of age is not true. You may lose some physical abilities as you age, but if you keep training, your mental abilities will not only make up for the physical, they will prove to be superior to them. In fact, you may come to discover that the mental and physical are not separated.

A Zen saying epitomizes how you can look at your martial arts journey: "When you reach the top of the mountain, keep climbing."

We can learn a great deal from this saying. It instructs you to have a goal, but to keeping moving after you arrive. It tells us not to set limitations no matter what level of skill you achieve or what award you've won.

Have your mind on a goal you want to achieve, think about it often, but don't be obsessed with it to the point where you think the achievement of it will make you happy. Simply practice and practice and practice and enjoy your life NOW.

Pay attention to the peak of the mountain but keep your mind focused on where you are every step of the way. Observe your breathing. Pay attention to the images running through your mind. See where you can challenge yourself to become more than you are right now.

I began stretching this morning shortly after I got up. After a few easy movements I went into a bridge and began to hold it for time. I was unable to do this exercise for the past couple months due to eye surgery, so I was far from being at my best. I set a goal to go for three straight minutes. But as the clock ticked I focused on the here and now by paying attention to my inhale and exhale.

After two minutes I began to notice how the exercise was getting harder. My neck hadn't been trained like this in 60 days. Instead of quitting I kept reminding myself, "Relax and breathe. You'll get where you're going sooner if you stay in the now."

"I Like to Climb"

Sure enough, three minutes arrived and I'd made it. I laid back and enjoyed the pleasant feeling. Then I went to the next exercise and repeated the same method.

Why do these exercises? After all, I don't have any plans to compete and I'm not trying to win any awards. So why train? I do it because it makes me feel good. But more than that, I do it because I like to climb.

Climbing to the top is great. It's exhilarating. But continuing on because you love what you're doing – that's when life gets really good.

When you reach your goal, the journey continues. Find another mountain to climb and learn to enjoy it more than the tallest mountain in the world. Keep climbing.

And as you climb, follow your breath. That's where the greatest mountain of energy rests. It's within you at all times. Keep following it, keep climbing. Keep breathing.

39

Laser Focus

*"You cannot depend on your eyes when
your imagination is out of focus."*

– Mark Twain

When I was in high school I refused to do anything that would reduce my focus on becoming a champion. No parties. No drinking, no drugs or wild nights.

As I got closer to the end of my senior season I began to examine the activities I was engaged in that I thought were helpful. I re-evaluated everything to see if it was moving me closer to or further away from success. In doing this I saw how I was wasting time on things that didn't produce. So I stopped doing those things and concentrated only on what I truly believed was turning me into a champion.

At the time my record was 7-4. After honing in I won 15 straight matches, qualified for the state meet on a severely sprained ankle, knocked off the defending state champion who hadn't lost in over two years, whooped the No. 3-ranked man in the state, and made it into the state finals.

Self-Congratulations

Then I began to think about how far I'd come. I began to pat myself on the back as well as feel negative about my next match. I went into the finals with half my heart and half a brain. I lost. And I never forgot the lesson I learned about losing focus.

Over a period of many years I had dreams about that match. Nightmares. I would awaken feeling a deep sense of regret. I let myself down. I failed. The pain of loss was still deeply etched in my psyche.

Why did I let up when I was so close? Why did I lose my focus?

The loss turned out to be a blessing as well as a warning. It taught me to keep my eye on the goal ALL the way to completion. It taught me to never get too absorbed with how good "others" told me I was.

Four years later, when I was in the NCAA II finals at Wright State University in Dayton, Ohio, I began to relive the same negative feelings before the finals that I had in high school. But it was different this time because I "caught" myself in self-destruct mode, got out of my seat and went to a quiet place where I could center and get focused.

I breathed, visualized – then fell asleep. I woke up 10 minutes before my match, loosened up and went on to victory.

Twelve years after that I was in Beijing. Once again I was in the finals. This time for the gold medal match in a world shuaijiao tournament. An hour before the match I felt emotionally rattled; I was nervous and fearful of losing.

But once again I caught myself faster. I didn't even need to leave the arena to gain control of my mind. Standing in front of the entire crowd, I began to breathe deeply. I pulled courageous, confident energy into my body and exhaled fear, worry, nervousness and panic.

Loss of Control

I focused primarily on my lungs and kidneys. Your lungs store the negative emotions of grief, sadness and depression. Much depression is caused by feelings of not being in control of your life. And when your emotions are in ebb and flow mode, you may feel you have no control. Yet, you do have control if you know how to breathe differently and form new mental pictures.

For more courage I pictured a Siberian tiger. It's a pretty fearless creature, don't you think? At 650 pounds it's able to run through snow drifts at 50 miles per hour.

Your kidneys house the negative emotion of fear. Ever go weak in the knees? Simply form a mental picture of death and destruction and while you're standing notice how quickly your legs begin to lose power.

If you ever feel weak in the legs, it may be fear holding you back. To counter this weak feeling, change your mental picture to an animal that is both gentle and powerful – a creature with powerful kidneys. Some people like to focus on a deer. I prefer a dolphin.

When you inhale courage and exhale depression, you gain power. And when you inhale gentleness and calmness and exhale fear, your inner power magnifies itself to a level that will surprise you.

How do I know? I know because after I changed my mental pictures and the way I breathed, I walked onto the mat and into the most magnificent zone I had ever felt in my competitive career. While competing for a world title, I was relaxed and at one with the world. I still couldn't go back and re-do my loss in high school, but I could use what I learned from that loss to win a far bigger and more important title. And that's exactly what I did.

Want laser focus? Then alter the way you breathe and what you mentally picture. See yourself at your best, larger than life. Feel yourself calming down with each breath. When you do this, you'll know the difference between going through the motions and giving it all you've got.

40

Laugh in the Face of Pain

"Pain is temporary. Quitting lasts forever."
– Lance Armstrong

I'm in the gym teaching a martial arts student how to use his bones like a knife. I'm showing him how, just by a change in thought, you can make your forearms feel like blades.

He's not seeing through the mechanics of what I'm teaching. He's only thinking about where his arm goes and where his foot goes. I grab him, toss him to the mat and teach him how I use my body like a saw.

"How do you do that?" he shrieks.

"I told you," I said. "I put an image in my mind of my body being something other than what it supposedly is. Then I let my body act upon that image." Later on, when I applied various holds he yelled, "Owww. Aaaah. Uhhh. Huuuh."

Finally I got tired of hearing him whine. I told him, "Alright, start over. Now this time there will be no whining. When I'm putting on these holds, you can smile and you can laugh and you can breathe – but there's no more, 'Owww, that hurts.' Got it?"

He nods. I put the first hold on and he started to say "Ouch."

"What did I tell you?" I warned.

"Sorry, forgot."

Two minutes later, after putting on the same holds, the guy is smiling and laughing. He's not feeling pain as he was before. Instead of putting on theatrics with his screaming, he's silently mastering his emotions, his thinking and his body.

I'll never forget the day my wife, Zhannie, rolled up the car window while her father's fingers were inside. He looked at her with a stoic expression, knocked on the window and pointed to his fingers.

Zhannie's eyes bugged out as she cried, "Oh no, what did I do?"

She pushed a button and rolled the window down. Her father, who was 65 at the time, removed his fingers and calmly looked at the indent from the window on his skin. Didn't say a word. Opened the door and got in.

I looked at him and smiled. He nodded.

Being Tough

My brother, Sean, told me how he taught his daughter, Erin, to be tough. When Erin was a child, like all kids, she would fall when running around the house. She'd bump her head or bruise her butt. And when she fell, Sean would stand at a distance and wait for her to get up. He would not rush to her aid with, "Oh, are you alright? Did you hurt yourself?"

Consequently, when Erin took up basketball, she was a different breed. Even though only 5-foot-4, as a freshman she guided her team to the state championship. And one of her secrets of success is what I call "Furey's Rule." It means: "no whining."

When many of the other girls got knocked to the floor, they'd stay down and writhe in pain for a minute. It wasn't like they had sprained an ankle or torn a hamstring either (a different situation). No, they simply fell and hit their fanny.

"When Erin fell," said Sean, "she'd just get up and look for the ball."

I laughed when he told me this. It shows, once again, that even in the face of pain, we are still in charge. We can rise above the pain. We can choose the direction we want to go.

Rising above pain involves making a choice to be a winner instead of a whiner. In your training, when things get tough, tell yourself you're not going to whine. You're going to have a "quiet mind."

Observe your reactions that showcase pain, but don't give in to them. Stay silent and keep your body relaxed. Do this in your training and you'll be amazed at how different life will be.

You'll learn to transcend life experiences at a level others will consider legendary. You'll have the tools that will help you create the life you want. Make a decision to rise above whining and complaining and you'll quickly see how much energy you used to waste.

Most importantly, you'll understand how laughing in the midst of pain is a trained skill, and one that serves you and others well.

41

The Element of Surprise

"He who has great power should use it lightly."

– Lucius Annaceus Seneca

I've spent the past month in China training with Master Liu. He's the man I wrote about earlier, who is the sole source of a treasured kung fu form, passed down from one master to one student, for over 2,000 years. For the form to survive, the master had to be somewhat psychic about whom he chose to carry on the lineage. If only one person received the knowledge, he couldn't afford to make a mistake when selecting his heir.

From the outside the form he teaches looks like other martial arts you've seen. The beginning looks a bit like Shaolin gong-fu; then it looks like Chen tai chi, and then it disappears before your comparative mind and becomes something you've never seen before.

Internal Power

The form shifts back and forth, the one constant is the internal power being exerted. You train and train and feel great in this system. Then you reach a point where you are drained – totally drained – and cannot go anymore. From the inside out, all the power you had was used up. Now you're ready for a hearty meal followed by a power nap.

The first form in this lineage has many benefits. I've been told it will help you live at least 10 years longer. That's a definite plus. Then there are the other promises of ridding your skin of age spots and wrinkles, eliminating toxins from the blood and excess fat from the waistline. Yet, perhaps the one benefit that will intrigue life-long martial artists the most is how this form gives practitioners *fa jing* very quickly – much faster than traditionally taught.

Fa jing is issuing or discharging power. The skill is kept under wraps and hidden from most martial artists, so it's probable you will train your whole life and never find someone who can or will teach you the true internal power secrets of an internal martial art. This is not a criticism of kung-fu, just reality.

Profound Concepts

One thing I love about studying Chinese martial arts is the way great teachers can explain energy in so many different ways. In the west we appear limited in terms of simple words to explain profound energetic concepts. Such is not the case in China.

For example, when I'm training with Master Liu, he talks about *jing* and *li* – different words to describe internal power – with every single movement.

"Ah, that is *bi li*," he says. Meaning you're using the force from your arms, not your whole body.

"You must turn from the feet, the knees, the hips and waist so that you issue *fa li* or *fa jing*."

Invisible Power

On other movements I am encouraged to use **an jing**, a power that is felt but not seen. Then there is *peng jing* or ward off power.

And how about *na jing*, an abrasive type of power in which your body feels like a saw.

Several years ago, I figured out how to use this **na jing** or sawing power with my rib cage and hips while grappling. I put my partner in a headlock and although all I appeared to be doing was holding my position, after he tapped out and we returned to our feet, I saw blood trickling down his face. I didn't realize this was going to happen when I used *na jing* in this way, and it shocked me when it did.

Training with internal martial arts masters is the best training you will ever get. It's the key to training over a lifetime and continually improving. It's a way that will show you how to outshine, with many different types of power, those who are much younger than yourself.

Those who only want to increase external power are missing half the battle, if not more. At some point, if the internal aspect is not developed, your physical body will fall apart. Amazingly, you don't see this deterioration happening to internal martial arts masters.

Regardless of their age, they still have grace, power and agility. They have many types of power, and most of them are hidden from view. The invisibility of their teachings makes them all the more precious. Unseen power is not only underestimated, but it contains an element all martial artists want more of: "the element of surprise."

Wise martial artists never underestimate an opponent based on appearances. After all, what you cannot see may be more than half the battle.

42

Smile in the Face of Fear

*"I don't run away from a challenge because I am afraid.
Instead, I run toward it because the only way to escape
fear is to trample it beneath your feet."*

– Nadia Comaneci

I was watching the tributes for Steve Irwin, aka "The Crocodile Hunter" on Animal Planet. Although I have always marveled at Irwin's bravery, I saw him use two martial arts principles on the tribute that made me hungry for more.

The first principle was with a rattlesnake Steve spotted in the Arizona desert. After sliding down a pile of rocks, he was face-to-face with a venomous diamondback. Yet, instead of showing fear, the Crocodile Hunter showed amazement.

One With the Snake

He smiled as he looked at the snake, then he grabbed a stick and slowly allowed the rattler to move toward his open hands. Next thing you know, Steve has the snake in both his hands, and the rattler's head is only a few inches from his face. When asked about the encounter, Irwin said he has no fear, so the rattler remains calm. He is "at one with the snake."

Later on in the program Steve is playing with an alligator and this brought up principle number two. At first he stays back, then gets a bit crazy and puts his hands in the water. The Crocodile Hunter was still in charge – or so it seemed. Then he put his bare hand (minus any food) out for the gator. Seconds later the gator catches Steve's hand between his jaws. Irwin stays relaxed, as if nothing happened. And when the gator pulled away from the river bank, Steve moved along with him, as if practicing push hands. An instant later the gator released his hand.

Go With the Flow

Irwin then turned to the camera, with his bloody hand clearly visible, and explained why the gator released his hand. It was simple: Steve didn't react in a fearful way. He didn't pull back. He went with the flow and the bite, and this caused the gator to let go because he couldn't feel that a battle of might and muscle was taking place.

In both instances Irwin was teaching us to be in control of our emotional state. How we feel in any given situation influences the outcome. To become great martial artists we must master our fears. And mastery of these fears begins with a deep awareness of our breathing, our posture and even our facial expressions. Everything we think and do sends out a signal that alerts others. If you're fearful, animals know it; so do human beings.

Imagine developing your skills, through practice, to the level that The Crocodile Hunter did with reptiles, snakes and other creatures. The only difference is that you do it with human beings.

Even in a life-and-death encounter, you can still carry a smile upon your face. You can still breathe deeply and remain calm. And from this vantage point, you can react and move at a far faster pace than when you are fearful, stiff and bewildered. Plus, with the right breathing, facial expression and level of physical relaxation, you can also escape from the seemingly inescapable.

There are many ways to practice overcoming fear. You can practice solo or with a partner. If by yourself, train before a mirror. Watch your movements and pay attention to your facial expressions. Do you have a stern expression? See if your jaw is clenched and your brow furrowed. If you have any facial expression other than a light smile or peaceful gaze, then go to work on that expression and soften it.

Pretend you're engaged in battle with a fierce adversary. As you picture the battle and see yourself moving, keep your calm, peaceful, smiling facial expression. The mirror is your partner.

Dan Gable and the author at a seminar in Tampa, Florida.

Let It Go

When you have a training partner, don't tell him what you're doing. Simply work on your skills and observe more than the movements of your limbs, torso, waist and hips. Feel whether or not your face is carrying tension. Relax and let it go. Breathe. Focus. Smile. And move.

Do this for a few weeks and you'll never go back to training without keeping these principles in mind. You'll be practicing much more than the externals of a martial art – you'll be practicing the strategies and tactics of a fearless warrior.

You may never choose to become one with poisonous snakes and ferocious crocodiles. But boy can we learn from the man who made it all look so easy.

43

Listen, Believe, Apply

"The best and fastest way to learn a sport is to watch and imitate a champion."

– Jean-Claude Killy

Dan Gable recently spoke at a seminar I held in Tampa, Florida. The 1972 Olympic champion wrestler and Olympic coach, who guided the University of Iowa to 15 NCAA team titles in 21 seasons (three of which I was a member), laid out his simple yet highly disciplined formula for success.

At the outset of his talk Gable said success boiled down to three principles. First, **you need to listen to good people**, people who are knowledgeable and want the best for you. Secondly, **you need to believe** in what you are taught by these people. Thirdly, **you need to apply** what you are taught.

According to Gable, you will succeed when all three principles of this formula are in place. And as you succeed, it will lead to DOMINATION if you continue working this formula. Not just becoming a winner or being crowned a champion, but **dominating** in your field, year after year, to the point where no one thinks he can beat you.

Think of how this formula applies to anything you want to master. Analyze the successes you've had and you will see they are directly proportional to how well you've listened, how much you believed in what you heard and how well and how often you applied what you were taught.

Listening and believing is not enough though. Nothing good is going to happen if you don't apply what you heard and believed. Unless you apply what you learned over and over again, unless you practice the art of *relentless repetition*, you will never become a success.

The Gable Formula

By using the Gable Formula, I can easily spot those who are destined for greatness and those who will never make it. Some students, for example, don't take notes, but they listen to every word you say. Others will take notes on almost everything you say, but they're not really listening. They're simply scribbling on paper. They're filling a pad with notes they'll never read again. Thus, no new beliefs are permanently installed in their minds.

Then there are those who take notes and apply what they've been taught. Thing is, they really don't believe anything you've taught. And so the person gives up at the first sign of defeat or the first dose of adversity. He stops applying what you taught because he listened but did not believe. It's the equivalent of learning various kicks, punches and throws then trying to do them on a more experienced person. Naturally, they won't work right away on someone with advanced skills. You need more practice. You need more time applying what you listened to and believed.

Follow the Advice

The truly great achiever listens and believes LONG before he ever sees the first sign of success. He follows the advice of his teachers. He applies the advice day in and day out, no matter how hard. Then, pretty soon he begins to see light coming through the tunnel. He sees that what he listened to and believed is true.

With this first sign of success in mind, the great achiever applies himself with even more belief. He listens even more intently because he sees a new reality shining through the clouds. He absorbs more knowledge and applies it as best he can.

If he never gives up, he'll eventually have his first big success. Now it's time for a celebration. Yet, potential danger lurks in the shadows. The achiever may begin to be filled with himself instead of with the subject he is studying. He may stop listening. He may still believe what he learned previously but now that he's tasted success, his mind can close and dismiss the teachings as if he's mastered them. I've seen it happen over and over again. Instead of the person staying open, listening to and believing even more than what he previously learned, he starts to lose what he gained.

The Gable Success Formula requires humility. It's hard to listen when you're pompous. It's hard to believe anything you learn when you think you already have all the answers. And if you won't listen and cannot allow yourself to learn and believe something new, then there is nothing to apply. With nothing to apply, there's no success.

Tack the words, "Listen, Believe and Apply" on a wall in your mind and in your home. Put this formula in a place where you'll see it everyday. Take a few moments to pause at what you're reading.

As you implement and achieve with this formula, others may ask you what you did to succeed. Be prepared. If you tell them to, "Listen, Believe and Apply," they may think this formula too simplistic to be true. And perhaps it is… for those who don't win very often. Dan Gable wasn't one of those who thought the formula too simplistic. And that's why he and his team won so often.

44

On Fathers and Father Figures

"The father who does not teach his son his duties is equally guilty with the son who neglects them."

– Confucius

My wife and I spend an average of 16 hours per week taking our children to various activities – from baseball to dancing to swimming, ice skating and piano. Oftentimes both of us are there to watch and show support for what they are doing. We do not simply drop the kids off and leave.

Being I don't take ballet or play the piano, I spend more time with my son than with my daughter. My wife and I believe this is not only good, it's critically important. And so, while driving my son to and from his practices, I talk to him about various attributes of success: desire, imagination, goals, having an "I CAN and I WILL" attitude. I relate success stories that were passed on to me by my coaches and teachers.

A Tragic Tale

I don't spend as much time with my daughter as I do with my son right now as I believe my wife knows how to raise a little girl better than I do – and I know how to raise a boy better than she does. Both

The author with his father, Jim Furey.

of us think it's tragic that young boys and girls today get less and less male influence.

One of the reasons so many men aren't manly today is because they had very little training from MEN. Their fathers worked all the time or showed little interest in their lives. Additionally, many of these men never found other father-like figures in sports or the martial arts. They never had male coaches who taught them how to be physically and mentally tough.

There are things a boy can only learn through transmission from his father and from father figures. Being tough, rugged and individualistic are the core of what a father is supposed to be teaching his son. A woman can teach these things, too, but it's not the same energy. Boys need a mixture of both energies, yin and yang. Right now, many boys are getting far more yin than yang and it throws their entire life out of balance.

When a boy whines, for example, a father needs to tell him to shut up and toughen up. When a boy cries, he needs a father who smiles at him and tells him to focus. When a boy gives it everything he has and fails, when his heart is broken, he needs a father who puts his arm around him and tells him he understands. He needs a father who will sit with him and explain that part of life is making mistakes and failing and those who become great are those who rise above the pain of defeat. He needs a father who will tell him that if he continues to give it his best, he will be a success no matter what the scoreboard or scorecard reads.

A Mother's Role

A mother's influence is huge; no man can ever offer the type of love and affection a child receives from a devoted mother. The same goes for what a devoted father gives his children. Whether or not he realizes it, his mere presence gives his child an energy that no woman can provide.

There are many children in today's world who are growing up without a powerful father's influence. This is where sports and martial arts can play a major role. Whether the coaches are male or female, if they're good, they know what being tough is all about. And mental toughness is what so many people can use more of today.

A Desire to Succeed

One of the principles I teach my children is how virtually everything in life boils down to having a burning desire to succeed, backed up by a willingness to enthusiastically practice as long as necessary to become great. Everything is whittled down to what you're picturing in your mind and how you feel about what you pictured. It's a good idea to have this message delivered to your children with both yin and yang energy. First people need to hear this message, then they need to see it in action.

Teaching isn't just talking; it's living what you teach. It's being a model for what you believe in. It's being involved with your children.

More men need to wake up and realize how vitally important they are to their children. More men need to take an active role in helping raise boys who are powerful, strong, dedicated, disciplined, compassionate and balanced. We've never had a shortage of women willing to do their part. It's time for more men to do likewise.

If more of us are fathers to our sons and father figures to others, we'll see a positive change in the way young boys become men.

45

Good to Great

*"Sports serve society by providing
vivid examples of excellence."*

– George Will

Looking good at what you do is important. Everyone wants to look and feel great while performing. So pay attention to your movements when you work as well as when you train. Pay attention to how you breathe. Observe your posture. Feel your feet connecting to the floor. Notice the movements of your ankles, knees, hips, spine, shoulders, elbows, wrists and neck.

When you do something, pay attention to your body and what it's doing. Do you hurry through everything you do so that you can't observe your mechanics? You can always add speed later on. At first, it's better to have a move down correctly and slowly. Once you can do something slowly and fluidly without mistakes, then speed is easy to add into the equation.

At Your Own Pace

Slow your movement down if your form is sloppy. There's no reason to go fast just because you've seen your teammate or a high-level teacher move at blazing speed. Go at a pace you can master, then upgrade.

A man wrote and asked me if he should do the bodyweight exercises I teach in **Combat Conditioning** fast or slow. He wanted to know if it would be appropriate to add pauses to his Hindu pushups and squats at the top, middle and bottom.

The answer is "YES." All variations are beneficial.

Perhaps today you'll do your exercises at normal speed. Tomorrow in slow-motion. The next day with pauses. All roads lead to greatness, provided you are willing to get off your duff and do something over and over again.

When I train, much of what I do is posture holding for extended periods of time. Quite often I hold a single posture for 20 minutes or longer. And I hold various postures for at least an hour each day. This type of training is one of the keys to developing internal power.

When you hold postures for extended periods, you meet the tension in your body-mind head-on and learn to relax and pass it by. You develop incredible focus and concentration as well as awareness you never had before.

Ironically, holding various postures helps you to move with grace and power. You learn to align your body properly and the correct alignments lead to better overall movement throughout the day, regardless of what you're doing.

Ballet dancers hold postures for time and no one ever questions the grace, flexibility and power these performers exude. So the same holds true when an athlete practices postures for his chosen sport or martial art. Once you've mastered the basic alignments of your body, you can go faster. But if you're like most people who slouch, slump and hold tension in their bodies even while at rest, this will interfere with your performance in any endeavor.

When you hold a posture or move slowly you're able to stand back and observe yourself. In so doing you might think, "What if I held the ball this way or what if I grabbed him by his fingers instead of his wrist? I wonder if that would make a difference?"

Knowing the Technique

Then you go back to the drawing board and you practice the refinement of your technique, and you practice it slowly once again, even though, for all intents and purposes, you already know the technique.

Yes, you do. You know it the old way you were doing it. Once you add a variation, you don't know it until you can pull it off in your sleep or while wearing a blindfold.

The difference between the good, the great and the master level of skill lies in your willingness to stand back and observe. The more you do it, the more you question yourself, the better you will become. So pay attention to your posture and your form – and keep doing so for the rest of your life. This is how you go from good to great.

46

Picture Your Previous Victories

"We all carry mental scrapbooks, but instead of preserving the joyous occasions of life, the moments of accomplishment, some people save only their times of failure and frustration."

– Dr. Maxwell Maltz

Most people visualize by sitting back, relaxing, closing their eyes and imagining what they want to achieve. This, no doubt, is a must-learn skill. That's why I continually stress the importance of doing a mental exercise called **Theatre of the Mind**, which I learned from Dr. Maxwell Maltz, author of the self-help classic, **Psycho-Cybernetics**.

Even though visualizing with your eyes closed is important, success oriented people also learn how to imagine with their eyes open. Once you can relax on command with your eyes closed, and once you are able to really feel yourself where you want to be, begin visualizing with your eyes wide open and integrate it into your training.

When I visualize, most of the time I don't need to close my eyes to get results of a startling nature. I don't need to think about going into a delta or theta state. I don't need to put on special high-tech glasses or listen to a metronome. I simply need to be able to tune everything and everyone else out, while mentally picturing doing what it takes to perform at my best.

A few years ago I was watching the Cowboys and Seahawks in the first-round of the NFL playoffs. During the final two minutes it looked like Dallas was going to win. They drove the ball down to the 1-yard line. All they had to do to take the lead was make a chip-shot field goal.

Tony Romo, the quarterback for the Cowboys, kneeled to receive the snap from the center. It was a good snap. Romo caught it and... oh no, the ball slipped from his grasp. He immediately picked it up and began racing toward the end zone. And he would have made it if a Seahawks player hadn't dove for his ankles and tackled him.

I thought about this situation a lot. Not only did I feel badly for Romo – no one wants to see a star quarterback go through the embarrassment and humiliation he must have felt – but I feel, based upon my athletic and martial arts experience – that prior to receiving the snap, Romo's mind was fighting off mental images of failure. And these mental images of making a mistake came to life in front of 60,000 screaming fans.

Martial artists can relate to situations like this. We know that when the fight comes to us, there's no time for sitting in a chair to visualize.

Eyes Wide Open

You've got to picture what you want and ACT immediately. And you've got to be able to do this with your eyes open. You must put a cancel stamp on all negative thoughts and see what to do in such a gargantuan way that nothing else can possibly enter your mind.

Now, let's forget about competing or using our skills to defend ourselves. Instead, let's think of another situation in which you feel fear or nervousness. For many, public speaking may come to mind. Speaking before a group of people terrifies many people more than the thought of death.

Yet, if you take a person who is afraid of speaking in public and observe him, you may witness that he has no trouble at all speaking to people one to one, even two to one or eight to one. Yet, this same person never thinks about the fact that he can speak, and speak well, to people in those situations. Instead of recalling past successes, he thinks only of possible failure. Instead of activating his internal success mechanism, he activates his internal failure mechanism.

But if this person becomes aware of what he does when he succeeds as a speaker, even if it is only to one or two people at a time, and if he thinks about those experiences and decides to do likewise in front of a larger group, his confidence will soar. In short order he'll be able to speak publicly with the same flair he uses when talking to one or two people at a time.

Human, After All

Back to Tony Romo. He's human like the rest. All of us screw-up. It's part of life. But the faster we let go of our mistakes and focus on what we've done in the past that led to success, the faster we will rise above our blunders.

There is a reason you never want to count out some fighters. There is a reason some martial artists always seem to find a way to win, even when things look bleak. And that reason has a lot to do with what he is picturing in his mind when the chips appear to be stacked against him.

What have you done before successfully?

Take a moment to recall your past successes, then blend them into your future. Don't focus on previous failures, unless you want more of them. Focus on previous victories, no matter how big or small.

Do this and you will begin to experience an unstoppable feeling of success. You'll be surprised at how often this feeling leads to getting what you want out of life.

47

Power in the Joints

"When you unlock your joints, your muscles gain a lot more slack immediately."

– Matt Furey

I took my normal station in a park on China's Hainan Island, where I like to train when I'm getting some much needed rest and relaxation. Groups of men and women practicing tai chi, chi kung and long-life exercises surround me.

A lady in her mid 40's stands nearby. We are doing similar exercises although we've never spoken to each other or trained together. She is my inspiration as she moves with tremendous grace, poise and power.

It may be difficult for some to see where power and flexibility go hand in hand. Often the two are considered separate. You're either flexible or you're powerful but you're rarely both. Such is the case if you've trained the wrong way. It is not the case if you've learned at the feet of a master for a long time.

Martial Arts Flexibility

Over a dozen years ago, when I was getting a private lesson from tai chi and kung fu master Ted Mancuso, we talked for a spell about the truths and falsehoods of flexibility training. There is no sharper contrast than the Chinese and Western world's approaches to flexibility. Sifu Ted stressed the importance of both strength and flexibility – not one or the other. He also stressed the importance of functional, mobile joints being the key to pushing your martial arts skills to another level.

In the U.S., most people think of their muscles when they think of flexibility. And when it comes to people's perception of flexibility, the most common idea is doing an exercise like the splits. Yet, in China, it's not the splits that matters. It's having loose, flexible joints and long, relaxed muscles.

Fittest and Strongest

The lady I so greatly admire training nearby spends no less than 20 minutes doing nothing but joint loosening exercises. She's an amazing site to behold because she's the fittest, strongest and most flexible lady in the park, yet she spends what others may think of as an inordinate amount of time on exercises like neck rolls, hip rolls, ankle, knee and shoulder rotations.

The author stretching.

There's nothing particularly difficult with what she does, yet these are the areas where most people are weak. These are the areas where most suffer injuries. The same people who may be able to do the splits or easily touch nose-to-knee in a hurdler's stretch have creaky and cranky joints. As a result, when they need to really expand, to really open up and move, they can't.

Seeing this lady do more advanced joint-loosening exercises is something special. If the average person observes her thrusting her neck and spine to and fro, I think they'd have a panic attack. Yet she moves back and forth, segmenting the various sections of her spine in a way that would make a belly dancer proud. She claps her hands before her chest, then rears backward and claps them behind her back. Not at the lower back and hip level either. She claps them behind her back at chest level.

Easy for her to do, you might think: she's thin and gaunt. Not so. True, some Chinese are less than 100 pounds, soaking wet or fully clothed. A great many are not. I assure you this lady is well muscled with calves that pop like bulges through a sack of potatoes. Yet none of her musculature interferes with her range of motion.

Fluid Power

Most importantly, there is fluid power when she moves. Everything flows. When she walks, she is connected to the earth beneath her feet. I've never seen her engaged in more than a handful of stretches that are mostly for the muscles, yet I am certain her muscles are very flexible.

Ralph, a 50-plus year old man told me that he recently began doing the joint loosening exercises I teach in my **Combat Stretching** program (available at **mattfurey.com**). He began doing them to heal his ankle. To Ralph's surprise, doing ankle rotations improved his shoulder. Within a couple sessions the shoulder was no longer hurting him.

Ralph also had trouble making a tight fist. When he tried there was a hole large enough to fit a pencil. Again, within a couple sessions of doing joint-loosening exercises, Ralph could make a tighter, more powerful fist than ever before. He was amazed. Greater mobility in his joints caused him to regain power throughout his whole body.

Remember this the next time you think ankle rolls and shoulder rotations are rinky-dink exercises. These basic joint-loosening exercises may not look difficult, but they're fundamental to your health and longevity.

The author training with pro wrestler Ian Hodgkinson, aka Vampiro.

48

Pushup Poker

"When I'd get tired and want to stop, I'd wonder what my next opponent was doing. I'd wonder if he was still working out. I tried to visualize him. When I could see him still working, I'd start pushing myself. When I could see him in the shower, I'd push myself harder."

– Dan Gable

When I was a college wrestler we used to do a workout called "Pushup Poker" that we learned from Coach Dan Gable. T'was very simple to explain, but much harder to perform. It pushed you to the brink of exhaustion (especially if you did it in the sauna), but if you did it religiously, you were sure to build an abundance of chi from all the deep breathing, along with a stockade of strength-endurance.

The workout goes like this: Draw a card. If it's a number card you do the number of pushups on the card. Face cards are a bit different, and as you might imagine, the joker is WILD.

For face cards, the jack, king and queen were 15 reps while the ace was 20. Depending on who was putting you through the deck and how cruel he was at the moment, the joker could be as many as 50 pushups.

Gotch'a

In 1999 I learned a variation of this same workout called The Karl Gotch Bible (KGB). Instead of doing regular pushups, you did much more. You performed Hindu squats for the red cards and Hindu pushups for the black cards. The same rules of Pushup Poker applied to how many reps you'd do for each card.

The KGB workout breaks up the monotony of a pushup-only routine. The Hindu squats hit the same muscle groups you normally work while in the horse stance. Additionally, the Hindu pushup is very different from a regular pushup because it incorporates the downward dog/upward dog poses from yoga, as well as a lot of stretching and flexing of the shoulders and back. So it hits you in areas that you cannot touch with traditional pushups.

When I first learned this routine from Karl Gotch, he would stand over me as I struggled. He would make comments like, "What's a matter, college boy? Didn't you get strong enough from weights to do these simple exercises?"

Wrestling Treasure

Karl Gotch, originally from Belgium, competed in the 1948 Olympics in both freesytle and Greco-Roman. Then he traveled all over the world as a professional wrestler. He spent many years in Japan where he was known as **Kami-sama** – "The God of Wrestling." But he was much more than the typical pro wrestler of today. After the Olympics he trained in submission wrestling (catch-as-catch-can) in England, and as a result improved his skills dramatically. He was given a black belt in judo after one workout and while living in Japan, he frequently trained in both judo and jiu-jutsu.

Karl was one of the few pro wrestlers from his era who truly knew how to grapple like the old-timers. To his contemporaries, wrestling wasn't just a sport, but like shuaijiao kung fu and Inner Mongolia's boke, it was also considered a form of self-defense; a martial art.

Even though Karl believed wrestling was a form of self-defense, he also preached that conditioning was your best hold. This is true not just in wrestling or martial arts, but virtually any sport. Today we see evidence of this even in sports like golf, which many may have believed didn't require much in terms of fitness.

In my ground-breaking book, **Combat Conditioning** (available at **mattfurey.com**), I cover many of the exercises Karl taught me, exercises that have helped martial artists and combat athletes of every variety, as well as fire fighters, police, the military and the average man or woman who wants to be fit.

Once you're able to do the basic exercises in my book, you can go the extra mile and get the workout of your life with the **Matt Furey Exercise Bible**. Inside you'll find a deck of cards with four core exercises instead of two.

Once you can go through the entire deck of cards, you'll know you're on your way to getting into the best shape of your life. And you'll understand the power of pushups and other bodyweight exercises.

49

Remember to Remember

"Imagination is more important than knowledge.
For knowledge is limited to all we now know and
understand, while imagination embraces
the entire world, and all there ever will be
to know and understand."

– Albert Einstein

This morning my son, Frank, walked into the bathroom when I was shaving. He noticed a running stopwatch next to the sink.

"Daddy, what are you timing yourself for?" he asked.

"So I get you to school on time," I said. "I'm giving myself four minutes to shave. If I don't time myself I may take too much time and you'll be late because of me. The timer keeps me honest so that doesn't happen."

After shaving I walked into the living room and saw my daughter, Faith, waiting for me.

"Let's go. Let's go," I said. "Get in the car now. We want to be on time. I'll be out in a minute."

My kids marched to the car and got in. I followed.

On the way to their respective schools I talked with them about the power of imagination and how they can imagine themselves getting smarter and smarter – learning faster and faster, improving more and more. I talked about SEEING the report card they want with the marks they'd like written all over it.

Imagination Rules

I talked to my son about seeing himself as a great athlete. "Everything begins in your imagination," I told them. "Imagination rules the world."

I can assure you this was not the first time I have told my children this. Nor will it be the last.

Repetition is paramount to success. And something that is valuable can never be repeated too often. First, you plant the seed, then you water and fertilize it.

This is what you do when raising children; this is what you do when you practice the elements of any skill. It's called "practice" for a reason. The very word implies that you never arrive. You are always practicing. You're always on a journey. And no matter what you practice, ultimately, if you've trained with the right intention, you end up in the same place as all the other winners.

Reinforcing Good Things

It's not coincidental that many of our greatest achievers can rattle off a string of their favorite maxims, from memory. Ever wonder why? It's because they continually reinforced the good things they needed to learn. In almost all cases, they did not hear something from their teachers once. They heard it repeatedly. And after they heard it they repeated it to themselves until it became a powerful life-altering belief.

Some examples I still recall from my early years of training are:

a. Your whole body is a fist.

b. Do not move as Mr. Smith and Mrs. Jones. Move as one unit.

c. When a baby cries, his whole body cries. When a baby grabs your finger, the rest of his body is perfectly relaxed.

d.   Any strength over-extended becomes a weakness.

e.   Being relaxed does not mean being limp. It means you're in a ready state of awareness.

f.   You've got to relax before you can EXPLODE!

g.   Be like a horse with blinders on.

When John Wooden, the great basketball coach at UCLA who guided the Bruins to 10 NCAA titles in 12 seasons, was in grade school, his father gave him a card entitled:

7 Suggestions to Follow

1.   Be true to yourself.

2.   Help others.

3.   Make each day your masterpiece.

4.   Drink deeply from good books, especially the Good Book.

5.   Make friendship a fine art.

6.   Build a shelter for a rainy day.

7.   Pray for guidance, and count and give thanks for your blessings each day.

Practicing the Basics

Wooden kept the card with him until the day he died. Such a simple thing, really. Daily reinforcement of the basics can and will take you all the way to the top. Why? Because so much of being successful is remembering what to think and what to do. Most people forget far too soon.

The great ones don't forget to remember. They remember to remember.

Remember that.

Oh, about that stopwatch. I don't use it every day. But when my wife is out of town and I'm playing the roles of both mom and dad, I really need to remember to remember. When there's no room for slack, it comes in handy.

The author practicing chi kung before Eiffel Tower in Paris, France.

50

Breathe Like a Samurai

"Deep breathing alone has made many a weak man strong and many a sick man well."

— Martin "Farmer" Burns

In 1914, Martin "Farmer" Burns created a by-mail course, **Lessons in Wrestling and Physical Culture.** In this course he talked about deep breathing and its positive benefit in the development of health and strength. What this fellow Iowan wrote could just as easily have come from the ancient Samurai of Japan or the Chinese masters of kung fu or tai chi. Or the yogi masters of India.

In the 1903 book, **Japanese Physical Training**, author H. Irving Hancock, wrote:

"The ancient samurai was accustomed to going out into the open air as soon as he rose in the morning. There he devoted at least 10 or 15 minutes to continued deep breathing, standing with his hands on his hips in order that he might feel the play of his muscles."

Breathing in the open air was recommended by Farmer Burns, as well as early American fitness pioneers such as Charles Atlas, Bernarr MacFadden and Paul Bragg. These men truly knew what they were talking about.

Lack of Breathing

In today's world, deep breathing isn't emphasized nearly as much. And even when it is taught it isn't placed in the proper light. The first skill a student must learn is how to integrate deep breathing with physical movement. This alone can easily double his endurance as well as help him avoid injury.

I'm in China right now enjoying my summer break, and each morning, just like the Samurai and the old-time physical culturists in America, men and women are up before the sun rises, doing chi kung and other deep breathing exercises. Unlike most exercise methods, where the focus in mostly on the muscles, the focus amongst the people I train with is mostly internal.

Earlier today I "played" with a man who began studying police gong fu in his 40's. He's now 52. He put his arms out to demonstrate his skill. I put my open palms on his wrists and forearms to get a feel for his energy. While I was feeling the power he had within, he was simultaneously shocked to feel how relaxed my touch was. There was no detectable intent. He could not tell what I was going to do and when. Like water, my thought is to be soft, malleable and flexible. No matter what, I need to able to fold and move, be shapeless and formless.

Focus on Your Breath

After playing for a bit we began to discuss the key to being so relaxed. It boiled down to two things: intent mixed with breath. And the key to developing this was internal practice, relaxing deeply while focusing on the breath.

You can tell a lot about someone simply by observing how he or she breathes. It doesn't matter if it's a competition, solo practice or simply sitting in a chair meditating. In fact, I believe you can map out the structure of how a person lives his life by observing his breathing pattern. Shallow breathers tend to be shallow people. Deep breathers tend to be interested in far more than the superficial.

Also revealing is the sound a person makes when breathing, especially while exercising. Does he or she have a problem with being seen or heard? You'll know by whether or not you can hear the person breathing. Does this person breathe in a way that says, "life is a struggle" or in a way that shows how he is simply in "flow?"

Maybe you've never paid much attention to the subject of deep breathing. For the first 25 years of my life I didn't either. Yet, I assure you, life is much better when you're in tune with how you breathe.

Pay attention to your breathing. Make sure it is deep and full.

Do like the Samurai. Do like the chi kung masters. Spend 10 to 15 minutes per day practicing. During those moments, continually remind yourself that *your breath is your power*. Inhale deeply and focus on relaxing to the core of your being. If you persist you will eventually discover the keys to the "inner kingdom."

51

Connect the Mind to the Body

"An incomplete soul he is,
whose mind and body are two."

– Rob Colasanti

You wouldn't think that someone would have to tell you this. You'd think it's one of those common sense bits of wisdom. Well, as the saying goes, "Common sense is anything but common."

What I'm talking about is connecting your mind to your muscles. I'm talking about 'getting inside' your muscles as you train. I'm also talking about going beyond mere exercise to give yourself every advantage possible.

Next time you see someone walking or running along the road, observe his mind. Where is it? Inside his body or running around somewhere else? Is the person grounded or a scatter brain who is going through the motions? Now take a look at people as they move around in the workplace. Is the person in his body as he works, or somewhere else?

In most instances, you'll see people with a body-mind disconnect. They're moving their bodies, but they're not really in their bodies – at least not in any sort of enlivening or empowering way. Why is this?

First, because most people don't have specific positive goals to focus and channel their energy. Training without a purpose is not training; training with a goal in mind is real training.

The second reason is because the trainee has a lot of negative things on his mind (or in his body) and he doesn't know how to clear them – or needs help clearing them.

A third reason is because he doesn't practice chi kung, wherein he is continually learning to pay attention to his breath and the sensations that accompany it. Practicing chi kung helps strengthen the body-mind connection, as well as clear your energy field.

Emotions Run Wild

On the day of the finals for the shuaijiao world championships in Beijing, China, in 1997, my emotions ran the gamut from total confidence to worry and fear. One hour I would be radiating total confidence; an hour later I would start to worry about winning or losing. Then I'd be confident again; then I'd go into fear mode, concerned about all the things that fighters think about, no matter what their skill level.

The good thing was I recognized what was going on inside my mind and how it was affecting my body. And so, without anyone knowing what I was doing, while warming up I began to focus on my lungs and kidneys. I brought courageous energy into my lungs and dispelled the depressing energy. For my kidneys I brought in energy that was alert and calm and dispelled the fearful energy. And when I took the mat to compete, I was buzzing with belief that I would prevail. I was totally connected – mind and body.

When you have a body-mind disconnect, your sense of power is severely restricted. You're unplugged. You're going through the motions but you're not really involved. And when your mind is not engaged in your activity, you won't get the results you want.

Work of Art

Along with the exercises I do each day, which are always rooted in engaging mind and body as one (our normal state), I also like to get worked on by massage therapists and acupuncturists. On a regular basis I get both because they help deepen the body-mind connection. When I get worked on, not only am I staying ahead of old injuries, I'm also getting the energetic pathways opened up wider so I can receive more energy from the Universe.

If you've never had acupuncture or deep tissue massage, I can assure you it is a powerful experience. Fact is, we have many stressful emotions, events and people in our lives, so it helps to ask for help from someone who can move you along faster.

Well, now you've been told. There are no more excuses. I've given you a number of ways to strengthen the connections in your body. It's up to you to pursue them and show the world you've got common as well as uncommon sense.

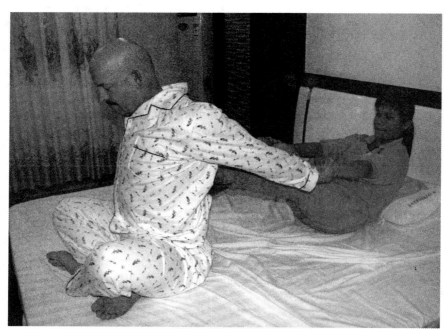

The author being stretched during a Thai massage session in China.

52

Slaying Demons

"Demons of self-doubt are always looking for minds to disturb, souls to drive mad."

— Matt Furey

On a trip to Finland I noticed "floaters" and other watery substances in my right eye. At first I thought it was no big deal, something I would sleep or rest off. After two days, however, I could no longer see with my right eye and knew I had a serious situation on my hands.

I contacted Dr. Thurber, my ophthalmologist, and he told me to take the next flight home. Meanwhile he got hold of one of the top eye surgeons, Dr. Howard Fine, who was waiting for me when I arrived on a Friday evening, long after everyone else, including all other staff, had gone home.

The surgeon determined that I suffered a detached retina, most likely because of eye trauma experienced over many years. So surgery was scheduled for the following morning at 10. It lasted two hours.

No Training

A day later the patch covering my eye was removed. I was told not to do any vigorous exercise for a month, and no martial arts training for two months.

I asked about walking and light stretching and was given the go ahead, but nothing that would increase my heart rate dramatically.

Okay then, what about practicing my martial skills in my imagination? I figured this would be a good thing, especially before bed at night. I could not do anything physically so this was a good way to enhance my skills. The doctor agreed this would be good for me.

So there I was, lying merrily in my bed, resting my limbs and pondering a brighter future. Then, sometime before the stroke of midnight, a demon of self-doubt began to disturb me.

"Furey, who do you think you are?" they questioned. "You're never going to recover from your eye surgery. You're never going to regain your vision. You're never going to rise above this. Face it, you're finished."

I was stunned to hear such voices playing in my imagination. I thought such negative thoughts were long gone. But now, in a moment of weakness, they were back. I was caught off guard and didn't know how to react.

"Look at you, you can't even fight back, can you?" railed the demon. "All bedbound and helpless, needing others to take care of you. I thought you were supposed to be some kind of master. I thought you were the guy who teaches others to be strong. Look at you now in your weakness."

At this point I struck back. In the theatre of my mind, in my imagination, I stood up in bed and struck the demon in the throat. Then I wrist locked him and slammed him to the ground. He tried to punch me in the head as I did this. He rose to his feet again, but I was ready. I stepped forward and hip tossed him on his head while separating his elbow. He shrieked.

I remained calm, still doing my Zen Master deep breathing, even in the midst of a fight. The demon then drew a sword and took a whack at me. I evaded his strike by falling to the floor. Then I grabbed my bathroom towel as he was preparing his finishing strike. I snapped him in the eye, kicked him in the gonads and pulled away his sword. Then I went to town on him in a way that would make a Samurai proud.

I laid back down, still doing my breathing exercises. Still calm.

Slicing Him to Bits

Eighteen minutes later another demon showed his ugly mug. As he started to yell I used the power of imagination to fight him. I drew an imaginary sword and began slicing him to bits.

Amazingly enough, he was even easier to beat than the first evil predator. No, I am not hallucinating. I am not delirious. I am alive. Let me explain. Whether or not you realize it, each day the demons of self-doubt, fear and worry are looking for resting places. They're looking for minds to disturb, souls to drive mad. Don't give them your mind as a resting place. Fight them off in your imagination and they'll bother you no more.

In the real world, remember how this same skill applies: Whenever anyone tells you that you "can't," draw your imaginary weapons and reduce their insult to the gutter realm where it belongs. More importantly, whenever you have self-doubts, fears and worries, be not afraid. Picture them as demons of doubt, then bag them up and toss them away.

Nothing, and I mean NOTHING, can defeat you but yourself. If you are on your side, then you've joined forces with the stranger within who wants to see you make the most of your life. And if you ever notice a fluid substance floating in one of your eyes, see a doctor.

53

So You Want
to be a Master?

"The more I practice, the luckier I get."

— Gary Player

The most successful martial artists, combat athletes and fighters I know are never content to rest on their laurels. They are continually refining what they know. Hour upon hour is spent in mental, as well as physical practice, looking for a minor tweak that may take a skill and transform it into something better.

One of the all-time greatest practitioners of this "never-stop-learning" habit was my wrestling coach at the University of Iowa, Dan Gable.

In many ways, Gable's skills were unparalleled. Yet, he lived by something called, "The Principle of the Slight Edge." In his world, "A technique that is perfect must be further refined."

Why is this so? It is so because a perfect technique does you no good unless you can execute it perfectly more often. It's all about more positive results more often.

Perfect is Not Perfect

Gable spent time each day watching technique videos, studying the latest books and analyzing competition. He frequently kept a yellow pad nearby while at prestigious tournaments to make notes. And he brought those notes into the practice room when we trained.

I'll never forget the time he came back from a tournament in the former Soviet Union. He was there as the head coach for the U.S.A. team, and while coaching he took pages of notes.

When Gable returned to the States and re-entered the wrestling room he began going over each detail he discovered in Europe. To the team's amazement he was executing moves that we'd never seen before, and he was doing them, at least from our vantage point, flawlessly.

How Gable was able to watch something at a tournament, make note of it, then perform it so effortlessly amazed us to no end. I told a fellow coach on the squad how stunned I was and he said, "Gable has been at this game so long that he's literally like a human sponge. He soaks everything up, even when he's not trying. He notices details that no one else even sees. That's why he's a true genius in this sport."

When I heard this said about Gable I made a mental note; a note I have never forgotten. That note mirrors what Michael Masterson, of **Early to Rise** fame (**www.earlytorise.com**), teaches regarding the four different levels of skill: incompetence, competence, mastery and virtuoso.

A Virtuoso

Here's how it plays out: Because of the time Gable had already put into the sport of wrestling (at that time it was already more than 20 years), he could literally implement what he observed – and do so with very little practice. Gable is a virtuoso.

Wouldn't you like to reach the virtuoso level of skill in your chosen field, too? Well, you can if you follow a couple guidelines.

Listed here are some of the guidelines I have used as a martial artist, combat athlete and businessman. Study this list and consider how it applies to your situation.

1. **Stay open-minded, no matter how good you are. No one has reached the point where he can no longer learn something new or further refine what he already knows.**

2. **Ask questions. When you see a skill being performed a certain way, ask yourself questions like:**

    Why is he doing it that way?

    Do I know for a fact, from actual experience, that what he is doing is good? Bad?

    What would happen if I tried it?

    Is there a better, easier, faster or quicker way to do what he is doing? If so, what is it?

3. **When practicing – literally be "outside yourself" observing what you are doing.**

4. **After practice, look back upon what took place and determine what your flaws were and what you can correct. Also look at what you did right and think of ways to do the right technique more often.**

5. Most importantly, **spend time each day thinking and working toward the level of skill you want to attain, then get to work.** You'll need about 1,000 hours to reach competency. If you want to go beyond competency to mastery, you'll need 10,000 hours. And if you want to become a virtuoso, well then, that'll require a lifetime commitment.

Either way you slice it, some will think that it takes too much time, even to reach competency. That's fine by me, and by you, I hope. After all, the fewer people there are who spend time working, the easier it will be for us to move up the ladder of success.

So you want to be a master? Perhaps you've set your sights too low. A virtuoso is even better.

54

Vengeance or Virtue?

"What you are thinking, what shape your mind is in, is what makes the biggest difference of all."

– Willie Mays

When I was 20 years old I lost a wrestling match to a guy that I didn't like too much. I wanted to beat him so badly I could taste it. Afterward, I came up with an idea on how I would get revenge the next time we competed against each other. As I thought about my plan I remembered a conversation I'd had a year earlier with one of my coaches.

"Vengeance has no virtue," he said.

"What do you mean?" I replied. "I really want to beat this guy. Isn't wanting revenge the best way to motivate myself?"

"No, it's not," he said. "The best way to win more is to focus on yourself and your skills. Focus on developing yourself to the best of your ability. When you compete, don't think about revenge. Think about doing your very best. This will carry you to more victories than revenge ever will."

After recalling this advice, I changed my attitude and focused on myself and my skill level. I learned to stay relaxed, and the next time we competed, instead of fighting him like a maniac, I stayed calm. In this mental and physical state, I moved much faster and countered his every move. I won simply by being aware of what I was doing to win, not concerning myself with revenge.

What this coach taught me so many years ago is advice I've heeded in my business. Sometimes reluctantly. Other times after doing things the wrong way first. In every case of revenge, even when justified, I got hurt more than the person I went after.

Over the last few years I've known a few people involved in bitter lawsuits. They've asked my advice on what to do. They've heard me speak about forgiveness; how vengeance has no virtue. But what to do when someone deliberately wrongs you? Does this philosophy apply then, or is it only for the arena or battlefield?

What's the Best Advice?

Now, just so you know, some of these situations are complicated. One involves assault with intent to do great bodily harm; the other involves the parents dealing with the death of their 19-year old son, who was murdered. What do I advise in these situations? Just walk away? Just forgive them?

Yes and no. I do not advise people to walk away, but I do advise them to pursue justice instead of vengeance.

Just as a martial arts master may have to use his skills to protect himself or his loved ones, he does not do so in anger. In fact, in order to fight effectively, as the feeling of anger surfaces, it is redirected until calmness and a feeling of relaxation reign supreme.

If a martial artist is challenged on the street, he can choose to walk away or in a spirit of calm, quickly put the encounter to an end. He need not get angry to subdue the attacker. He only needs to be aware of what is happening and act in an appropriate way. Last time I checked, we fight better when we're aware of our environment as well as our actions and emotional state.

This same martial spirit or martial awareness can be brought into the court of law. For the family who lost their son in a tragic incident, they can choose to walk away or seek justice through the legal system.

A State of Calm

The emotion of revenge will only further complicate and destroy their lives. It will tear them up while they're going after the other party. It's far better for them to pursue justice and their legal rights while in a state of calm.

"Revenge and justice are two very different things," I told them. "Revenge is a desire to punish on a personal level. Justice is taking appropriate action in a fair way. Don't confuse the two. You can pursue justice aggressively – and win without harming yourself in the process."

Revenge cannot bring happiness, even though people pursue it for the feeling of happiness they hope to get from it. In the end they will neither achieve sufficient revenge or a lasting feeling of happiness about the verdict. And that's why vengeance has no virtue. It cannot make you happy.

55

Give Yourself a Clean Slate

"Don't let yesterday use up too much of today."
— Cherokee Indian Proverb

This morning I was getting a bite to eat at a restaurant when the waitress came by my table and muttered something. As she's waited on me many times before, I looked her way and said, "Huh?"

"New day, same old shit," she said. Then she pushed her index finger in a downward manner, as if pressing a rewind button. "Everyday is like a recording," she added.

I smiled and said, "Naaaah."

Her day brightened a bit even though I appeared to be disagreeing. Truth is I DO agree with her. SHE is reliving each day as if it's the same. Yet, when I go to the same restaurant and am waited on by her, each instance is totally new to me. Even if I order the same food, it's still a new experience. I don't bring the same old Matt to the table each day. I bring a new Matt, someone with fresh aspirations and inspired ideas.

New Day – New Experiences

The experience in this restaurant is no different than what I conditioned myself to have when practicing a combat sport or martial art. Every day is a NEW day regardless of whether or not I am practicing the same forms or moves.

To become good at anything you need to practice what you want to master thousands and thousands of times. Yet, with each repetition, if you bring a fresh energy and perspective, you will never get bored. You'll never feel like you're hitting the rewind button. And you'll never say something like, "New day, same old shit."

One of the biggest reasons why people have trouble succeeding is simple: They won't let go of their negative past.

Instead, they recall, relive and dwell on all the negatives.

Negatives like:

- Previous failures.
- Negative opinions of others.
- Fears and self-doubts.

New Instructions on the Board

All of these negatives are like old chalk left on a blackboard. You can remove it by taking an eraser and wiping the slate clean. But this is only going to happen when you are WILLING to do so.

In order to erase the old chalk, though, you must do MORE than wipe the slate clean. You must also give yourself new instructions on how to live.

These new instructions are no different than another set of words you would read on a blackboard or computer screen, with ONE major distinction. These words are positive. They are pure and powerful. And they're designed to take you where you want to go. They're not designed to keep you stuck in the past.

There is a time and place to recall the past – but it's the positive past that needs to be recalled most of the time; the past that, when focused upon, causes you to create MORE success experiences.

Each night, before I go to bed, I make sure I wipe my slate clean. I wipe away the mistakes, failures and setbacks. I wipe the slate clean even if I think it doesn't need it.

Why? Because I know that forgetting to do so makes for a slate filled with notes that someone else placed on the board, and chances are that "someone else" doesn't have successful intentions for me. Be clear about this. YOU rule your roost, no one else. So don't let anyone put negative notes on your board.

Don't Wear Dirty Socks

Sakai Yusai, considered a Living Buddha in Japan, once told me that each day is like a soiled pair of socks. You wouldn't think of putting on dirty socks to begin a new day, so why carry yesterday's troubles into today? Toss the dirty socks in the laundry and make today a breath of fresh air.

Give yourself a clean slate before you go to bed each night and the dawn of a new day will shine in your mind for all to see.

56

Where Everything Starts

"Genius is 1 percent inspiration and 99 percent perspiration. As a result, genius is often a talented person who has simply done all of his homework."

– Thomas Edison

Everything in the Universe is either improving or getting worse. And that includes any skill you're currently proud of. My life changed the day I learned this. I originally thought you could reach and maintain a certain level of skill. Yet, this very notion defies natural law. The only constant we maintain is continuous movement. We are either moving forward or we're losing ground.

Practice, Practice, Practice

In China, you see the top martial artists training each and every day, rain or shine. There is no such thing as "overtraining." It's practice, practice, practice – not so much for the attainment of a prize, but for the JOY of training itself. Going deeper inside the movements is often the only goal, and I'll be the first to say it's an admirable one.

I realize that each movement, each morsel of know-how we are taught can be developed to the depths and breadths of the ocean itself, if we entertain the idea that there is always more.

It's easy to say, "I know that already" when we see something being performed. Yet to know is to execute, and execution can always be improved.

Acute Awareness

How? Ironically, we improve most not just by "doing" – but by being aware of what we're doing. We can take a deep look at what we're doing, working on a skill and observing our level of focus and intention.

This is why it is important to closely observe what we do each and every day to improve our skills. Whether it is hard physical training, meditation or chi kung is not as important as the awareness you bring to the lesson. Greater awareness leads to improved skills; lack of awareness leads to deteriorating skills.

To be at your best, think about how you communicate with yourself; how you use your imagination; how you breathe, how you tense or relax your muscles; how you resist another's force or go with it; what you picture in your mind; and how you talk to yourself.

Recently I worked out with a teacher of Shaolin gong-fu who wanted to learn some submission holds from me. After several minutes of talking we began to spar in a friendly manner. He was stunned at how "soft" I was. When he grabbed me there was, in his own words, "nothing there." Nothing to fight against and nothing to feel coming at him. No wind-up; no recoil. Most surprising to him was how I never grabbed him; how I moved him without clinging; and how I controlled his limbs even though I didn't grab him.

He wanted to know how I was able to move powerfully without appearing to use power. I told him deep breathing mixed with relaxation, something we do automatically as infants. Not the mechanics of deep breathing, but more like the awareness of deep breathing while moving. Keeping my mind on my breath and off everything else.

I told him if he wanted to develop even greater skills he must be more than a mechanic who follows movements. He must go deep inside the breath and deep into the movements he makes. He must rid from his mind the idea that he knows everything – or anything. Instead, he is to dwell on how much there is to learn, even when we think we know a lot.

There is nothing in the Universe that cannot be improved, even that which is simple. We attain mastery not by striving for it, but by paying attention to where we are; by thinking about doing a little bit more each day, and by realizing how everything starts and ends with the breath.

57

Your Imaginary Training Partner

"You can't put a limit on anything. The more you dream, the farther you get."

– Michael Phelps

I was giving a seminar in Pennsylvania when a student asked, "How do you continue to improve when you can already beat everyone in the practice room? If there's no challenge for you, can you still get better?"

Tis a great question – and one that the great masters have always had to answer. After all, once you rise above the herd, if you rely on your partners for your continued growth, you're not going to improve much. The key is SELF-RELIANCE, not partner-reliance.

Fighting Yourself

You can always get better if you view yourself as your greatest opponent. And when you view yourself as your biggest adversary, you can stage battles against yourself in your imagination, and act these battles out when you train. Whether you call it shadow boxing, shadow wrestling, kata or form practice, I truly believe it is the key to continued improvement in anything. But ONLY if you use your imagination in an empowering way and truly "go within" while you train.

In **Psycho-Cybernetics** (for more information on this program go to **www.psycho-cyb.com**), Dr. Maxwell Maltz wrote about teaching shadow boxing to salespeople, young baseball players and public speakers. In each case, performance improved dramatically.

In my seminars I've taught shadow boxing to people of all walks of life. I teach the principle of the exercise: acting or role-playing a future event as if it's happening now. The positive results have been stunning. Professional musicians come alive. Stock brokers make better trades for their clients. Surgeons perform flawlessly in the operating room.

Sadly, many people today just don't get it. Martial artists think real training is sparring and fighting with a partner, and anything without a partner is a waste of time. Salespeople think that calling on someone is all you need to do. But what about getting mentally prepared before the call?

Almost all successful people will acknowledge that success is at least 90 percent mental. Yet, they cannot explain how to use the 90 percent. All their advice pertains to the physical 10 percent.

Every great master I have ever known in any endeavor spent a great deal of his training time by himself. Even the master chef usually cooks and experiments alone.

When I'm in China I always look for the man or woman who is off in a corner, training alone. He's not part of a group. He may teach classes or give private instruction, but when it's his own training time, he's by himself.

Watch THAT person and you'll usually see a very high level of skill on display.

Drilling on Your Own

In college I often marveled at the amount of time Dan Gable spent on his own, drilling moves by himself. Regrettably I didn't figure out that this was one of the biggest secrets to mastery until I was finished with my collegiate wrestling career. At least I figured it out afterward. Most people never get it.

It's one thing to go through the motions of a form or a technique. And it is nice to see all the outward mechanics of a movement down pat. It's great when you hear others observe you from across the room saying things like, "Wow, that's beautiful."

When someone is truly great, you can sense beautiful energy when he's barely moving. He may be holding a position and you note that he looks different than others holding the same stance. He may look your way and you'll notice that there's something unique going on.

At a youth baseball game the other night, a happy-go-lucky man was told to stand on one team's side of the fence to bring them good luck. People noticed that whenever this man sat on one side, that team would do well. And as soon as he moved to the other side, or even in between the teams, the team that was doing well would crumble.

Oddly enough, this man spends a lot of time by himself and is always in a joyful state. He uplifts others wherever he goes without even trying.

The Quality Rises

An experienced artist knows when someone is really, really good. He can usually tell with a quick glance from across the room.

But how did he get so good? Practice is the biggest part of the answer, but ask the great one how much of his practice time was spent alone, late at night or early in the morning when no one else was around. You might be surprised at the answer.

I'll never forget the advice a wrestling coach gave me years ago, when I was better than anyone else in the practice room. "Make sure you don't take it easy on any of your training partners. Beat them up as bad as you can, every time. If you take it easy on them your skills will go downhill. You'll start getting sloppy."

I did as instructed and my skills continued to improve. Yet I'm sure if I had spent even more time training with my "shadow self," my skills would have transcended those I was developing with mediocre training partners.

If you spend time each day battling your imaginary self – or doing battle with other imaginary foes, you will be amazed at how much value and SKILL you develop. Your imaginary partner reigns supreme.

The author receives a private audience in China with the Shaolin monks.

58

Find Your Success Groove

"In sports, mental imagery is used primarily to help you get the best out of yourself in training and competition. The developing athletes who make the fastest progress and those who ultimately become their best make extensive use of mental imagery. They use it daily as a means of directing what will happen in training, and as a way of pre-experiencing their best competition performances."

– Terry Orlick

Late last night I went out for a ***dao zou*** chi kung walk, only this time I had a friend along. Typically I don't talk as I train, but this session was different as I had a message to relay. As we headed out the door I began telling my friend how the average person is completely unconscious of his day-to-day habits and thinking, and therefore is unable to recreate success over and over again.

"What do you mean?" he asked.

"Well, this may sound odd, but when a major celebrity agrees to an appearance, there is often a lengthy contract that goes into illustrious detail about what he or she wants the hotel room to be like. It'll state what kind of bed, what kind of robes, what kind of soap, water, and so on the celebrity wants."

"Okay," he said, showing interest.

Success Experience

"And this may seem very strange to the average person," I continued. He might think, "What a prima-donna." But the major celeb may be making all these requests because he knows, in great detail, what creates a success experience. He also knows, if he's been paying attention, what creates a failure experience."

As we continued to walk I went into greater detail: "Take myself, for example. One of the things I figured out as a competitive martial artist and wrestler was that I needed to get up early and go for a run on the days that I competed in a tournament, especially one that began in the morning."

"I came to this conclusion after competing in a number of tournaments wherein my first match was abominable. I felt like I was still asleep during the match. I was cold and stiff. And my lungs burned like fire because they weren't acclimated to the cold air in the arena. And so, after performing poorly a couple of times I figured out that some early morning running and sprints, performed outside in the cold, would open my lungs and get my entire body-mind ready for battle. This one simple change in pre-competition habits catapulted me to the top in tournaments I would have probably not won. I realized how powerful this habit was so I repeated it before every tournament, regardless of how important it was. Doing the early morning sprints helped me find my success groove."

"No one else on the team that I'm aware of ran in the early morning, the same day of a tournament. For whatever reason they didn't need to. But I did. I understood what I needed because I paid attention to what works, did more of it, paid attention to what didn't work and stopped doing it. Failure to follow what works always spelled disaster. Choosing to do the things that get you into your "success groove" will make it seem as if you cannot fail."

"That's amazing," he said. "I never thought about it that way before, but now that I do, it makes perfect sense."

Keep Track

Whether it's sports, business or any other creative endeavor, this same type of structured thinking applies. If you keep track of what you did and what you thought on the days you were at your best, and if you keep repeating those words and deeds, you increase your chances for success dramatically.

So keep track of what works, as well as what doesn't work. Repeat what works. Discontinue what doesn't work. Even if others think your requests are strange, even if others think your habits a bit odd, you'll know your secret to finding your success groove and they still won't even know there is one.

59

The Powder of Champions

*"The message I wish to convey is please live each day
as if it is your entire life. If you start something today,
finish it today. Tomorrow is another world.
Live life positively."*

– Sakai Yusai

A great sage in Japan was visited by a fighter. The fighter was afraid of losing and asked for guidance. The sage told him not to worry, not to be afraid. He said he had a powder that would make him unbeatable. He told him it made everyone else he gave it to unbeatable as well.

The fighter listened intently. The sage then gave him the powder and told him how to mix it with water each day. He said that if he drank it in water before his fights he would be assured of victory. This powder would give him strength, speed and stamina. It would make him invincible.

For many years afterward this fighter was unstoppable. He never lost a single bout. He was absolute perfection, just as the sage predicted.

The Real Powder

Then one day the fighter visited the sage to ask for more information about the powder. He wanted to know why it was so powerful and what was in it that made it so effective. At this point the sage asked the fighter to follow him. The sage led the fighter to a shed where food supplies were stacked. He reached into a sack, grabbed a handful of powder and let it fall from his hands.

"This is the magic powder I gave you," said the sage.

The fighter drew close to the sack and proceeded to read the writing on the bag. Before the fighter could open his mouth the sage said, "It's flour. I gave you flour used for baking."

"You gave me what?" said the fighter. "Flour?"

"Yes, I gave you flour," said the sage. "And this proves that you won the fights because you believed the powder gave you everything you needed to succeed. But you could have succeeded without the powder if you believed as much in yourself. According to your beliefs you have achieved victory. Now go back to training and believe in yourself as much as the powder and victory will still be yours."

Secret Formula for Success

Amazing story, isn't it? And it's so true. Everywhere you go you will find people who believe they have the championship technique, teacher, formula or food. And these people will swear up one side and down the other that something other than oneself is the reason for victory.

There is no doubt that teachers, techniques and foods can and do play a role in our development, but when push comes to hard shove, the fact of the matter remains that it is YOU who is the decider.

You, alone, make a decision as to what you believe and what you accept. And no matter how good the teacher, the system or the secret food, if you don't believe you're good enough without it, you probably aren't.

"I am Just a Man"

On a recent trip to Japan I met with esteemed marathon monk, Sakai Yusai, who is considered a Living Buddha, a living saint, for doing the unthinkable, running 1,000 marathons and double-marathons within 7 years, traipsing through the hills of Mt. Hiei near Kyoto. Less than 50 monks have completed this task in over 100 years.

When I met with him I came to express gratitude for the positive influence he has had in my life. In reply he said, "I am just a man. You did it yourself."

A great sage, he is.

Although he could have taken the credit I was giving him, he put the focus back upon me. He dumped out the magic powder.

Of all the things I've learned from all the many great teachers and coaches I've had, one that will remain with me forever is, "I am just a man. You did it yourself."

The real powder of champions is not a powder. It's the thoughts you think, the way you breathe and the way you move. Think, breathe and move like a champion and the world is yours.

60

1% More

"That's one small step for man,
one giant leap for mankind."

– Neil Armstrong

A coach wants you to give your best effort. So what does he do? He tells you to give him "110 percent."

Not much has changed in my mind since I heard a coach use this line the very first time. In fact, I'm still trying to wrap my noggin around what 110 percent would look or feel like.

Think of it this way: If at the highest levels we're only using about 10 percent of our mental capacity (and sports are mostly mental games with physical attributes), then why would I need to give 110 percent? Seems to me if I was able to give 11 percent, I would move to the head of the pack.

A 1% percent bump in performance is much easier to imagine than 110 percent. Former NBA coach Pat Riley figured this out long ago, when he was with the Los Angeles Lakers. After the team had already snagged an NBA team title, he re-motivated them by getting every single player to commit to a 1 percent improvement in one area of the game.

This 1 percent commitment led to staggering results. Just by being able to see the possibility of giving 1 percent more than the previous year, caused several players to improve 20 percent or more.

Asking the same players to improve 20 percent over the previous year wouldn't have worked as they couldn't have pictured how they could improve that much. But when Riley talked about a one percent improvement, he cracked open the door of possibility. One percent was the wedge he needed to motivate the players.

Don't Give Me 110%

In my study of Chinese internal martial arts, the focus is never on giving 100% of your very best. Why? Because when you try to give 100%, you add unnecessary tension to your body-mind, and this tension doesn't improve performance.

Several months ago I was warming up my son, Frank, in the bullpen prior to a game. Unlike other days, he was way off in his throws. The balls were flying over my head. Or wide right followed by wide left.

I walked up to him and reminded him to inhale deeply and let the exhale go. Prior to this reminder, Frank was barely breathing. And if a pitcher isn't breathing deeply with each pitch, he's holding onto tension.

By getting Frank to inhale and exhale deeply, his accuracy improved dramatically. No more balls over my head, or to one side.

After getting him to breathe deeply I added some other internal martial arts knowledge to his pitching. I gave him a specific percentage of his maximum I wanted him to be using when he threw the ball. I based this percentage upon what I know will give Frank maximum velocity and control.

I can assure you the percentage I gave him was NOT 100 percent, much less the much heralded "110 percent."

Guess what happened?

He started throwing perfect strikes to me. And they were stinging my hand. Let me tell you, when a 10-year old throws hard enough to sting and adult's hand, he's got some pop.

The author stretching 1% more on a banyan tree in Singapore.

Remove the Tension

When Frank took the mound a few minutes later, he looked great.
He effortlessly threw one bullet after another. Three up – three down.

Every pitcher has good days and bad days. It's rare that one who is doing poorly can be turned around on the same day. Yet, it can be done regularly if you know how to get the athlete breathing properly, remove his tension and get him focused with empowering mental pictures of success.

Last month I worked with several other pitchers – all of whom are beginners. None of these kids could throw a strike when we began. But after a few minutes of changing their mental pictures and getting them to breathe deeply, they were throwing strikes.

Each boy went home believing in himself a little more than when he started. And this belief will result in improved performance.

Keep in mind that I did not work on the mechanics of any of the pitchers in any way. All I focused on was how they breathed and how they used their minds. That was it, and it was enough to change the location of their pitches.

Ridding your body of tension is key to superior performance. It's key to getting the most out of life. It's key to turning wild pitches into perfect strikes.

The Gateway to Greatness

Success isn't about giving 100 percent or 110 percent. It's about learning to get more out of yourself while feeling like you're doing less. It's being in a relaxed-ready state that allows for the natural flow of effortless output.

Tension interferes with performance. It creates physical, mental and spiritual resistance. You're much better off with zero resistance; zero interference from your body-mind.

When you can get someone to commit to a one percent improvement in anything, you open the gateway to greatness.

61

Your Great Leap Forward

"When you improve a little each day, eventually big things occur. When you improve conditioning a little each day, eventually you have a big improvement in conditioning. Not tomorrow, not the next day, but eventually a big gain is made. Don't look for the big, quick improvement. Seek the small improvement one day at a time. That's the only way it happens – and when it happens, it lasts."

— *John Wooden*

Back in 1995, when I got started as a writer, I didn't have a goal to write a book in a weekend or in a week to 10 days. I started with a much smaller step: a much smaller idea. I decided to write four double-spaced pages per day. That was it.

By following this strategy, I wrote my first book, **The Martial Art of Wrestling**, in 10 days. So how did four double-spaced pages per day turn into a book 10 days later?

Very simple. Once I got into the writing of those four pages, I would get lost in the shuffle of time and before I knew it I had written at least 10 pages.

Even so, the next day I'd sit before my computer screen and start again with my daily goal of writing four double-spaced pages. And once again, without consciously trying to write more than four pages, I usually did.

When I have advised my students to begin the same way, they are almost always successful. But if four pages is too big a task for them to swallow, I knock it down to two pages… or one. If one page is overwhelming to the student, I'll knock the daily task down to a paragraph, or a sentence. Whatever it takes for the person to mentally nod and say to himself, "Okay, that's something I CAN do."

How can this small-step approach lead to a book? Well, if someone starts with a goal of writing one sentence per day, he will organically begin to write more than one sentence. And he'll do so without pressure, prodding or external motivation. It will simply happen.

The same goes with a health and fitness regimen or any other endeavor.

The Journey of a Thousand Miles

On a flight to China several years ago, I was reading the book review section of USA Today. It featured, *One Small Step Can Change Your Life* by Robert Maurer. The book teaches how to apply the Kaizen Principle of small, incremental improvements in business as well as our everyday affairs. Sounded like a winner to me, so I got a copy to see how I could begin applying this principle in my own life at a higher level.

As I read the book I became aware of a couple truths. The first was that everything I have started on and succeeded in, began with the "one small step" approach.

The second was that almost everything I have tried to make a "Great Leap Forward" on has resulted in me eventually setting the task aside for a better day, which usually never comes.

Why People Don't Get Started

Upon thinking things through a bit longer, I surmised that a lot of people never get started toward the achievement of a goal because the time commitment or work involved seems too great. If they choose to plow ahead anyway, ultimately, within a few weeks the person gets discouraged and finds excuses why he or she cannot do it.

My goodness. Do you realize that I have just described roughly 90% of the population?

And so, when you hear me talking about getting "one minute of exercise per day" – or one minute of writing, understand that I am giving you a solid strategy for success.

Why? Because anyone can successfully complete one minute of something. After you're done with one minute, you probably don't even recognize it yet. This means you're now working within a groove. Once inside this groove you'll start feeling better and you'll naturally begin adding more time to the activity.

For example, if you get up in the morning and find yourself conflicted about exercise, or writing, or cleaning, or selling, I have a quick and easy cure for you:

Start With Very Small Chunks of Time

If you don't think you have enough time to clean your home or office, then commit to cleaning for one minute. Get started and see if you can stop in one minute. I bet you can't.

How much could you improve your life if you took a small step each day on something you've been putting off? How much could you change your life if you did the following each day...

One minute of exercise.

One minute of deep breathing.

One minute of cleaning.

One minute to learn a new word or phrase.

Smiled and said hello to one person.

Read for five minutes.

Wrote one paragraph in a journal.

Honestly, how much could you change your life if you stopped expecting a Great Leap Forward each day and instead, you simply took care of the "small stuff?"

Want to know the answer? I'll give it to you this way. If you do the small stuff each day, and you do it over and over and over again, it won't be long before people will think you've made a Great Leap Forward.

62

Hate to Lose

"The difference is almost all mental. The top players just
hate to lose. I think that's the difference. A champion
hates to lose even more than she loves to win."

– Chris Evert

There are two reasons champions train longer and with more focus than others. They love to win. And they hate to lose.

Champions love the sweet smell of victory. After winning, many champions feel more spiritual, more connected, more ALIVE than at any other time. Everything else in life goes pale in comparison to the thrill of entering an arena to fight the fight of your life, and winning, amidst the cheers and energy of a crowd.

Winning has many external rewards. Not only do you win ribbons, medals, plaques, trophies and certificates, but you often earn the respect of those who otherwise wouldn't pay attention to you, including the media. If they care enough about you and your accomplishments, you get to see your name, face and heroics in print. Perhaps even on television.

Driving to Victory

With that said, there's another truth about what it takes to win and this truth is usually not taught or understood by the masses. Put simply: Champions usually HATE to lose even more than they love to win. The hatred and pain connected with losing often drives them to win.

A few months ago I heard the following: Twenty percent of all athletes hate to lose. And 95% of all Olympic champions are in the hate-to-lose group.

True Inspiration

When I was 12 and began to really develop in the sport of swimming, I typically came home from each meet with four or five first-place ribbons. One evening, when I was getting ready for my fifth event of a dual meet, the freestyle relay, I saw that we were missing a teammate. We couldn't participate in a 4-person relay with three people, so I had to find a teammate, and fast.

Sitting along the fence was another 12-year old, Bill, who only swam in one event at every meet. I talked to Bill, told him we needed him to be the number three man in our 4-person relay.

"But I can't swim freestyle very well," Bill said. "I'm as slow as a turtle."

"Don't worry about it," I assured him. "If you just get across the pool and back we'll be fine because I swim the anchor leg."

Bill continued to object, but I insisted with great enthusiasm. And when the starter fired the gun, Bill was with us at the starting blocks.

Our team held a half-pool lead when Bill dove in to swim his leg of the relay. When he finished, I had three-fourths the length of the pool to make up in order to win.

We lost the relay that day. Afterward, Bill walked over to his parents. I followed, angry as a wild boar. I hurled insults at Bill, calling him every name in the book.

My Mother witnessed what was going on and called out to me. She told me we were going home. At first, I refused to leave, but she took charge and hauled me home... on foot.

As we walked, my Mom told me that all great champions hate to lose, but the truly great don't make a poor display after defeat.

"If you act this way," she said, "people won't appreciate how good you are. They'll say, 'Yeah, he's good, but he's a hot head.' If you ever act this way again, you're done with swimming."

From that moment on, the champions who didn't "show boat" after victory inspired me. And the great ones who lost but didn't complain publicly also caught my attention.

One of my favorite quotes on how to balance the pride of winning with the angst of defeat came, once again, from my college wrestling coach, Dan Gable.

He wrote: ***"There is no mat space for malcontents or dissenters. One must neither celebrate insanely when he wins, nor sulk when he loses."***

Without a doubt, this ideal is much easier to read than follow. Gable himself, had to learn to live by this maxim and although he did so, at times it was challenging.

In 1970, for example, after losing his final match in college to Larry Owings, which snapped his 181-0 winning streak, Gable sobbed publicly, hand over face, when presented with his second place award.

But after leaving the auditorium distressed, Gable used the pain of his loss as motivation. He not only avenged his loss to Owings in the Olympic trials two years later, but he won all six matches in the Munich Games without surrendering a single point. Gable will be the first to tell you that he used the pain of his loss to become a champion.

As a collegiate athlete, I saw plenty of wrestlers cry and pound their fists after suffering a humiliating defeat. I've seen trash cans thrown through windows. I've seen walls punched. I've seen brothers come to blows.

And I've seen Gable intervene by saying something like: It hurts, doesn't it? It's painful, huh? Well then, don't ever forget this moment. Don't ever forget this pain. Use it to make yourself better.

The great ones love to win. They expect to win. But boy do they ever hate to lose.

The author doing hill sprints in Evian, France.

Acknowledgements

As *Expect to Win – Hate to Lose* makes its way around the globe, I'd like to give thanks to all the forces who came together to make this book a reality.

First of all, a big thank you to Dave Cater, who served as editor at *Inside Kung Fu* for so many years. I thank you for taking me on as a columnist, for suggesting I put this book together and for doing the initial edit.

To my parents: Jim and Kathleen Furey, who helped bring me into existence and nurtured my desire to become a champion.

To Rob Colasanti, *Ambassador of the Martial Arts*, for your suggestions, edits and friendship.

To the two Vince's who helped put this book together: Vince Palko for the cover and Vincent Lai for the layout. Both of you are awesome.

To all the coaches I've had throughout my life, many of whom you read about in this book. To name all of them would be difficult, but let it be known that I'm one fortunate human being to have trained with and been coached by men like Dan Gable, Bruce Baumgartner, Mike DeAnna, J Robinson, Dr. Daniel Weng, Karl Gotch, Master Liu, Master Zhang DiYi and so many others.

To Zhannie, my wife, who encourages me as well as our children, Frank and Faith, to rise up and put forth their best effort. I love you and am grateful for all I've learned from the moment we first met. To all the athletes, martial artists and clients I've had the great honor to guide and instruct. Being your teacher has played a huge role in my life and I am sincerely grateful.

To Ted Nicholas, who helped get me rolling on this path so many years ago. Your ongoing encouragement means more to me than words can express.

To Dan Kennedy and Pete Lillo, for your marketing lessons.

To Tom Hanson and Paul Reddick, thanks for your friendship – and the lessons you give my son, as well as the Yankees tickets.

To all the dedicated coaches who've given lessons and spent practice time with my son and daughter. I am truly grateful to know they are surrounded by coaches who expect them to give it all they've got; coaches who know that becoming excellent at what you do is the quickest path to "fun" ever created in sports.

To Ed Baran, for the sensational websites you've created for me over the past decade. And last, but not even close to being the least, I tip my cap to Carol Brown and company. You've made major contributions to how things get done around here, freeing me to do what I do best.

Thank you, thank you, thank you... to one and all.

About the Author

Matt Furey was born in a small town in Iowa, named Carroll.

At eight years of age he began competing in swimming and wrestling and through dedicated practice became a champion in both. In 1981, Matt Furey was the state runner-up in the Class 3A Iowa High School State Wrestling Championships at 167-pounds. He attended The University of Iowa from 1981-1984, where he wrestled for Olympic Gold Medalist, Dan Gable, and was a member of three national championship teams.

In the fall of 1984, in order to help rebuild a doormat wrestling program, Furey transferred to Edinboro University of Pennsylvania, and in 1985 he won the NCAA II national title at 167-pounds, defeating two-time California state champion, Howard Lawson, in the finals. While at Edinboro he was coached by Mike DeAnna and two-time Olympic Gold Medalist Bruce Baumgartner.

In February of 1987, Furey opened a personal training business for wrestlers and fitness enthusiasts. Most of the high school wrestlers he trained went on to wrestle in college.

Furey began studying various martial arts in 1990 and immediately saw the physical, mental and philosophical links these arts had with wrestling. This lead to the publication of his first book and videos in 1996, entitled, **The Martial Art of Wrestling**.

Also in 1996, Furey began competing in the ancient Chinese grappling art of **shuai jiao**, the oldest style of kung fu. Furey's teacher, Dr. Daniel Weng, a national champion from Taiwan, and a ninth-degree black belt, guided Furey to three national titles.

During Christmas of 1997, Dr. Weng brought two U.S. teams to Beijing, China, to compete in the world championships. In Beijing, Furey won the gold medal at 90 KG (198-pounds), and was the only non-Chinese to win a title. In addition, Furey's world title was historic because it marked the first time that an American had won a gold medal in any world kung fu competition held in China.

In the spring of 1998, Furey was inducted into the Edinboro University of Pennslyvania Athletic Hall of Fame.

In 1999, Furey traveled to Tampa, Florida to train under the legendary Karl Gotch. Several months later Furey moved his family from California to Tampa, Florida, so he could train with Gotch full-time. Gotch taught Furey a treasure trove of knowledge on conditioning as well as the real professional style of wrestling, known as catch-as-catch-can (catch wrestling).

Furey's unique experience as a Chinese kung fu and wrestling champion, earned him covers for **Grappling**, **Inside Kung Fu**, **Karate Illustrated**, **Gladiator** and **Martial Arts Illustrated**.

In 2002, **Grappling** magazine dubbed Furey, "The King of Catch Wrestling" – and in the book Grappling Masters, Furey is one of 22 elite world class grapplers who are interviewed and featured.

In 2010, **Inside Kung Fu** named Furey as their **Hall of Fame Writer of the Year**.

A Sneak Peek at Other

Matt Furey Products

"How to Be Unbeatable in Anything You Do"

Forget the "bubble-wrapped, mamby-pamby" advice about success you're getting from almost everyone today. Listen to someone who's been there and done it. Someone who wasn't any good and made himself into a Champion – and applied the lessons he learned to every area of his life.

Dear Friend,

When I was growing up in a small town in Iowa, I wanted to get good at something. I wanted to stand out, to be admired, to get so good at something that when I walked by people would say, "There's the guy who..." If you're honest with yourself, I'm sure you can relate. All young people want to excel at something. For some it's sports, for others, music, mathematics, writing or art.

Then... LIFE happens. You have teachers or coaches who tell you that you'll never make it. You have classmates and "friends" who laugh at your desire. You may even experience conflicts inside your own family, with doubting parents or siblings.

And then what happens? In most cases, the young person gives up on his goals and dreams. He begins to doubt himself, to second guess his talents and abilities.

This doubt turns into fear and frustration. And as the years pass by, even though you've acquired news skills, abilities and talents, any time you attempt to tackle something new, the ghosts of fear, doubt, worry and frustration creep into your vision, and the keep you from getting what you want out of life.

"What happened to me?" you may ask yourself. "I used to be a person of confidence and courage. Now I doubt myself at every turn."

Two Different Groups of People

After Robert Fulghum, author of ***All I Really Need to Know I Learned in Kindergarten***, became a best-selling author, he was often asked to speak before two distinctly different groups of people. The first group was kindergartners. The second group was college graduates at their commencement ceremony.

When speaking to the kindergartners, Fulghum would ask questions such as:

How many of you can sing?

How many of you can dance?

How many of you can draw?

How many of you can... (fill in the blank?)

It didn't really matter the question. Whatever Fulghum asked, eyes filled with belief raised their tiny hands while saying, "I CAN."

Contrast this with the soon-to-be college graduates. When asked the same questions, nary a hand went up. The words "I CAN" were almost non-existent.

When I hear stories like this, I tend to wonder: I thought you went through school to get an education. You just finished 16 or so years of school. When you began you could sing, dance and draw – and now you can't???

The Greatest Motivator

A friend of mine often says that people today are so afraid of failure and defeat that they bubble-wrap themselves to avoid anything and everything that could make them feel bad.

And this bubble-wrapped mentality is being passed on to the youth of today, with dire consequences.

The other day a coach who works with my son asked if he could "ride" him harder.

"Your son has a lot of talent," he said. "Do you mind if I get on him and ride him to become better."

I said: "Coach, that would be great. I understand what it takes to become a champion, and babying someone isn't the way to get the job done."

"Thank you," he said. "You're one of only two parents who will allow me to give their son or daughter the edge they need to make it."

"Really?" I asked. "Are you serious?"

"Absolutely serious," the coach said.

"That's very sad," I replied. "Don't count me in that group. Put us into the group of two who are willing to be pushed. We want to get good. And if being pushed is what it takes, then push."

33 Years Ago

I'll never forget the day, some 33 years ago, when I was told I would never become good, that I would never amount to anything.

These comments were some of the most motivating words ever spoken to me. They forced me to dig deep, to make something of myself. These words challenged me.

I wanted to be a champion. I wanted to be good. And whenever someone told me I wouldn't be, it made me focus even harder to prove him wrong.

Additionally, whether I won or lost, I took inventory of myself. I asked myself how I could have done better. I looked for mistakes to correct. And then I got back to work.

A Mindset That Follows You

This mindset, this way of being, is still with me to this day. I didn't get left on the mats where I competed.

It followed me into the world of business. It followed me onto the Internet. It follows me when I go on stage to speak about success and achievement.

And it follows me, perhaps more so than anywhere else, in the gut-wrenching, edge-of-your-seat story I lay out for you in *The Unbeatable Man*.

Many who have read virtually everything I have ever written, have said that *The Unbeatable Man* is my best work ever.

Others who have been given *The Unbeatable Man* book and CD's from friends, and didn't know anything about me or the sport I wrote about, grabbed the book and were so completely hooked from start to finish, they finished in one sitting.

For example, here's what one baseball coach had to say about it:

"This book should be on the shelf of every winner's library. If you want to propel yourself to metoric levels of success and fulfillment then get **The Unbeatable Man** *right this second. It will catapult you to the top of the medal stand!! One of the best inspirational books ever"*

Paul Reddick
The Master of MPH
PaulReddickBaseball.com

And here's what an Aussie from Down Under had to say about it:

"Hey Matt,
G'day from Australia. Mate I am PUMPED! I just got my copy of **The Unbeatable Man** *in the post! I have already read the damn thing! It is an inspirational and mind blowing read. The strength of the mind is unquestionable. People MATT FUREY is the truth! Not only IS the book kick ass but the mind vibrations interview and bonuses that come along with it will floor you. As soon as I finished the book I hit a bodyweight workout straight out of combat conditioning! Ha-ha!*
Get this book. It IS the business. The **Unbeatable Man** *should be mandatory school reading world wide!*
Thanks Matt. You're the man."
Lachlan McIntyre

And if the comments listed above aren't enough proof, he's more:

"Matt Furey's exciting story reads like an adventure novel. He writes with the grace of Ernest Hemingway while his ideas and exciting message floor you like a punch from Jack Dempsey. This book is TOTALLY INSPIRED. It shows how we too can do this... we can be unbeatable like the hero of this book."
Steve Chandler
Author of Fearless

"Matt Furey is a master and a don of self-development in the deepest sense. No one on the planet can teach you better than him how to be truly strong and how not only to acquire the essential discipline to develop yourself to your full potential but to actually enjoy it. This lovingly told, beautifully written account of how he overcame all obstacles to become the great teacher and man he is, will instantly inspire you to make the best of yourself. It's brilliant. Read it."
The Barefoot Doctor
author of The Man Who Drove With His Eyes Closed

"The Unbeatable Man had me on the edge of my seat from start to finish. A riveting story of about desire, overcoming obstacles, blocking out the negative and the heartland work ethic. Gives a rare and unique inside look at small town America, including family and parenting. As I read I found myself looking back on my own 'glory days' and to my amazement, I found many similarities in how Furey and I were striving to accomplish the same, even though he wrestled and I played basketball. This book will motivate and inspire you."
Nick Nurse
NBA Coach

Matt Furey is a man that defies easy description. He has had an amazing, multifaceted life, including being a World Champion athlete as well as a bestselling author.

His writings have long been used all over the world as "study guides" for great copywriting and his rare interviews are eagerly studied by "insiders."

He is one of the rare ones who is generous, gracious and yet completely unafraid to express an unpopular opinion. He will fight for that in which he believes and strongly convince others to do what he knows is right. And they love him for it.

But it is Matt Furey's passion for studying people and life's principles that has permanently raised the level on which he vibrates. And this is never more apparent than in *The Unbeatable Man*.

The Unbeatable Man is an astonishing opportunity to see a man move from visionary to creator. As you read you will discover how he overcame unbelievable barriers. Sometimes the secret came in learning, other times it required taking a leap of faith.

And with each chapter of *The Unbeatable Man*, you will discover how YOUR barriers can be overcome; how a road to peace, satisfaction, and success can open before you where only obstacles appeared just moments before.

It is a first-of-its-kind publication with life-changing value for millions of people.

Dr. Trevor Neal
CEO, NaturalPharmacy.com

So Powerful It Should Be Mandatory In All School's Curriculum – Worldwide

"Matt, In the 5 years I have known you, I have been privileged to spend quality, private, one on one mastermind and mentoring sessions with you and I will forever be a student of the 'Furey Method... yet nothing and I mean nothing could have prepared me for the priceless lessons I discovered in *The Unbeatable Man*.

I devoured all 128 pages with more hunger than a ravenous dog devours a big, juicy steak. Once I started reading your story, I couldn't put your book down. It gripped my attention like super glue. For a few hours, the world stood still.

Never before has any one book inspired me, motivated me, brought tears to my eyes (due to my own childhood memories flashing back) and delivered so many life changing lessons until... The Unbeatable Man.

I truly believe your book, should be mandatory in the school curriculum – across the world, as your message will change people's lives and what better place to start than with children.

Your book isn't just for men, it's for women too and anyone who doesn't invest in *The Unbeatable Man* – is a bloody idiot!
Trevor 'ToeCracker' Crook – Copywriter & International
Public Speaker
www.TrevorCrookBlog.com

The Unbeatable Man is a riveting real-life story of how one man's dream, desire and focus beat all the odds against him to become a champion. You don't have to know anything about wrestling or sports to Ôget' this book. As soon as I read the 1st chapter, I was so sucked in by the energy and emotion of the story that I didn't put it down until I had read it from cover to cover. I was on the mat with the referee, in the stands with the fans. And I was INSIDE the mind of a Champion. The life changing nuggets of wisdom Matt reveals in *The Unbeatable Man* will inspire you and challenge you to go after your own dreams... and never, ever give up.
Carol Brown
Plant City, FL

I finished reading *The Unbeatable Man* book this morning. Wow! Holy smokes! Where should I begin? It's even better than Ernest Hemingway's The Old Man and the Sea! This book made me want to workout! Yep. Right now, I feel like training HARD! I'm totally pumped...and I intend to "beat the bag" here in a bit. It's kind of how I felt after I watched the movie Rocky for the first time. The lessons in The Unbeatable Man are timeless. And the central message is applicable to businessmen of all kinds. Athletes of every type. People who have had their tail whipped for any reason and need a high-powered pep talk, teenagers, martial artists, the military, etc. Virtually anyone will benefit from this book. The message is indeed a powerful one and the timing for it is perfect.
Rob Colasanti
"The Ambassador of Martial Arts"

"Matt Furey is the rarest of gurus: one that as I've studied in depth and gotten to know my respect for him continually deepens. I've known him for 5 or 6 years and spent many, many hours with him! I wish there was some way better than just my words to convey to you my years of experience learning from Matt so every cell in your body would know getting this amazing book is a no brainer."
Tom Hanson, Ph.D.
Author, PLAY BIG
www.PlayBigBook.com

The Way of Unbeatability!

Everyone, once you get past the defenses, wants to be significant, wants to be loved, admired and respected. Sadly, damn few people in society today ever show you the WAY. But *The Unbeatable Man* WILL. *The Unbeatable Man* will show you the way to make yourself UNBEATABLE. He lays out the groundwork for what you can and will become if you follow the same approach he used.

The Unbeatable Man teaches you how to strengthen your spirit, your inner being, to the point where regardless of how many times you've failed or fallen, you can still get back on your feet and MAKE IT HAPPEN.

In *The Unbeatable Man* you will discover:

- The hidden power of silence and how it can give you unstoppable power to reach out and achieve the impossible!
- **How to handle critics or anyone else who tells you "it can't be done" or "you'll never make it."**
- The right way to fight back if you feel that everything is against you or things aren't going your way.
- **What to be mentally picturing and imagining about your future in order to move forward with ease!**
- The correct response to fear!
- **The Dan Gable secret – it's something no one teaches, yet it catapults the average and ordinary to greatness incredibly fast!**
- What to do if bad things ever happen to you!
- **How to turn every disadvantage into an advantage, every negative into a positive!**
- *Plus much, much more all laid out for you in the form of a parable that makes the information STICK!*

Transform Yourself NOW!

The Unbeatable Man will help you transcend and transform yourself. He may help you become larger than life. Most importantly, he will help you get up after every mistake, every set-back, every knockdown until you've become virtually UNBEATABLE.

If you don't want this for yourself, then get it for your son or daughter, your niece or nephew, or a friend in junior high, high school or college who wants to be somebody but is continually tempted to give up his or her dreams in order to fit in and be liked.

Giving up who you are to be liked leads to emptiness. Sticking to your guns leads to feelings of personal power and invincibility.

That's why so many high-achievers have such high praise for The Unbeatable Man. They understand better than anyone how the principles in this book give you an edge over anyone and everyone.

Better Your Best

Praise for *The Unbeatable Man* has poured in from the day the book first launched. Best-selling author, **Dan Kennedy**, who seldom lends praise to anything, said, **"It's TERRIFIC."**

Steve Chandler, best-selling author of *FEARLESS*, wrote: **"This book is TOTALLY INSPIRED."**

But the comments I love most are from people like Ron, who told me his son, who won't read anything, grabbed a copy of *The Unbeatable Man* and read it from cover to cover. He couldn't put it down.

Be one of the first to place your order for *The Unbeatable Man* today and I'll send you a **FREE** copy of *The Power of Thought Vibration*, a riveting CD with a $49 value that you'll listen to again and again for ideas, inspiration and intestinal fortitude.

I look forward to hearing about how *The Unbeatable Man* and the **FREE** CD changed your life.

Best,

Matt Furey

Matt Furey

P.S. The most motivating, captivating and inspiring stories of all times, are usually those of young athletes who defied the odds. Everyone loves a WINNER! *The Unbeatable Man* is more than a book about winning, though. It shows you the way to the indomitable spirit that lies within you. Order NOW and keep me posted on your progress.

Puts functional strength into every fiber of your being...

"Combat Conditioning: The #1 Total Body Fitness System on the Planet – Simultaneously Turns You Into A Strong, Flexible, Butt-Kicking Machine"

Follow the Legendary Routine That Quickly Catapults Your Strength, Endurance and Flexibility to record levels. Feel the results that tens of thousands are raving about worldwide...

Dear Friend,

I was the total skeptic. Not only had I lifted weights for years, but after 28 years of being involved in sports and martial arts, at the national and world championship levels, I thought I'd seen it all.

So I just didn't believe it when Karl, a 76-year old former Olympian and trainer of legendary fighters in Japan, told me I could get into FAR better condition when I focused on bodyweight calisthenics alone. Keep in mind that Karl, the man who told me this, made the shift to bodyweight exercises when he could bench over 400 pounds and squat over 700.

At first I refused to believe him, but I couldn't shake the feeling that he was right. After all, I had read about the **Great Gama** of India, a wrestler who followed this same type of program and was unbeaten in 5,000 matches. In terms of size and strength, Gama was 5'7" and 260 pounds of streaming steel. And that was in the early 1900's – long before steroids.

I'd also heard that **Bruce Lee** did these same type of bodyweight exercises. And we all know about Lee's incredible ripped, lean, muscular look. Not to mention how lightning fast and fluid he was.

Not only that, but there was **Herschel Walker**, a Heisman Trophy

winner and All-Pro Running back who did 500 pushups and sit-ups each day. So that made me think even more.

The Converted Skeptic

After I made the decision to "give the program a try," I was hooked. I couldn't overlook the reality that within 10 minutes of my first workout, my body was cooked. I could barely do 25 Hindu Pushups, 50 Hindu squats or the Back Bridge.

But doggone it, did I feel GREAT. I felt better than I had after any other workout I'd ever done. I was pumped, stretched and energized – all at the same time. And I wasn't in pain.

Hi, my name is Matt Furey, and I'm the author and creator of the international best-selling *Combat Conditioning System*. I've been featured in major martial arts magazines around the world and have appeared on the cover of several. I'm also no slouch when it comes to having and using functional strength. You don't win a world championship in kung fu and a national collegiate wrestling championship if you're a weakling, nor do you easily change a program that's working. As the saying goes, "If it's not broken, don't fix it."

But let me tell you, when I was only 25 years of age (today I'm 48), my body was already starting to get broken from the programs I followed.

I had elbow tendinitis, knee and back pain, shoulder and wrist pain. I regularly visited a chiropractor to have my neck and back adjusted. I woke up in pain and hobbled around for the first hour of the day. On occasion my right knee would swell. I visited an orthopaedic surgeon and he suggested removing my bursa sac.

Again, all this by age 25.

So let me ask you: How good could a strength and conditioning program be if I had big muscles at that kind of expense? But you know what? Injuries from weight training, weight lifting and cardio are the norm, not the exception. You cannot say the same when you train with your own bodyweight.

A New You in 7 Days!

Within 7 days of following The Combat Conditioning System I felt like a new man. Aches and pains from years of training disappeared. My body got flexible where it was tight. Muscles that were and could not be helped with weight training, got super strong. I had power, strength, stamina and endurance, all at the same time.

And along with that another quality severely lacking in today's world: peace of mind.

Over the course of 3 months my body changed big time.

In fact, for your consideration, here are 12 of the most amazing benefits that I and tens of thousands of others have gotten from *The Combat Conditioning System*. I'm betting these are important to you, too:

1. I blow-torched off my excess body fat so quickly that I could eat more than I normally did and still look better than ever.

2. **I packed and chiseled functional muscle onto my legs, chest and back that I've never had before, even from weights.**

3. I simultaneously doubled my strength and flexibility – and did so without needing separate workouts.

4. **I quadrupled my endurance inside of 30 days. Just think how much this helped my sparring. No matter what, I NEVER get tired.**

5. The chronic back and shoulder pain I had from years of heavy squats, deadlifts and bench pressing went away within a couple weeks. And much of that pain had been with me for nearly 10 years.

6. **I sleep like a log. Eight hours of deep sleep is no longer a goal. It's automatic. As soon as I hit the rack I'm out like a light.**

7. My self-confidence grew by leaps and bounds.

8. **I can train anywhere. I don't need more than a few square feet of carpet or pavement and I'm all set. I have absolutely no excuses and my body is loving me for it. I don't need any equipment. Just my own bodyweight.**

9. I get a kick-butt workout done in 15 minutes or less.

10. **I've turned back the clock. My friends tell me I look 10 years younger than my age. Awesome!!**

11. I have an explosive type of strength that weights couldn't give me. My movements are super fast even when I'm just playing around.

12. **My muscles are like a pliable and powerful tiger – ready to pounce on prey in a heartbeat.**

So there you have it. The 12 reasons why *The Combat Conditioning System* is the best fitness program on the planet. But forget about me.

Take a look at what so many in the military have to say about *Combat Conditioning*:

Matt, I am a US Marine stationed overseas. I am also a wrestler/judoka and the Marine who developed the Marine Corps Martial Arts Program. I use your courses regularly. I like your no-nonsense approach. Particularly as I get older, bodyweight exercises are quick, flexible, all-encompassing and convenient. Keep up the good work!
Lt Colonel George Bristol – USMC

Mr. Furey, We have been applying the principle of 'mastering your own body weight' to our football program and have been pleased. A 12 – 1 championship season last year was our reward. Thank you sir.
Bonner Cunnings Yosemite, CA

Dear Matt, When I got your program, I changed my whole way of thinking about how one should train for Combatives. I am now totally off the weights, and, to tell you the truth, I have never felt better or been more flexible in my life. I feel great and have lost no size, strength, or muscle mass... as a result I scored the maximum number of points on the Army Physical Fitness test. HOOAH! You are doing great things, and I and the U.S. Army Officer Candidate School owe you a lot. TREAT'EM ROUGH!
CPT Judd D. Mahfouz – Infantry

Dear Mr. Furey, Let me say I have benefited a lot from both your **Combat Conditioning** *program. I*
am a Marine stationed on Okinawa, Japan and I do a lot of kickboxing and NHB fighting on the side. Your exercises have given me a tremendous advantage and combined with my other routines (shadowboxing, sparring, bagwork, wind sprints, and grappling drills) have gotten me into the best shape of my life.
LCpl Sandor Devenyi – United States Marine Corps

Dear Matt, Being a U.S. Marine in a field unit, I spend much of my time in Physical Training, and I'll admit, I thought that I was in peak physical condition. 2 months ago I began your **Combat Conditioning** *program and quickly realized that I had been missing something. While platoon PT consists of mostly running and incorporates some bodyweight exercises (i.e. pushups, pull-ups, crunches) I had been spending the bulk of my personal training time in the weight room, lifting heavy. It embarrassed me the first time I tried to do a reverse pushup and couldn't. I haven't set foot in the weight room in the last 2 months. My 3 mile run time has dropped to below 18 minutes, I've lost a good 10 lbs and my body fat has dropped 4%. You can see the difference and God knows, I can feel the difference. I've introduced the rest of my squad to your program. Thanks for helping us kick ass and take names in a hellish and unforgiving manner.*
D "Bubba" Byng – LCPL, USMC "Golf" Co, MCS Battallion

Change Your Body – Change Your Life

The Combat Conditioning System comes with a fully illustrated book with 48 extraordinary bodyweight exercises that get results faster than anything. Along with the book you'll receive 3 workout DVDs, including:

- DVD #1 – **The Leg and Lung Workout** (this will kick your butt into shape fast)
- DVD #2 – **The Pushup Workout** (this will be incredible upper body and core strength)
- DVD #3 – **The Ab and Back Workout** (flattens your stomach, energizes you and helps eliminate back pain)

If I were going to put a price tag on the value of what you'll receive from following the exercises in the *Combat Conditioning System*, I could easily justify $1,000.00. And this is no exaggeration.

The great news is that I'm not going to charge you $1,000 or $500 or even $250 for the information in my program.

Right now, for the next 200 people who respond to this offer, I'm only going to ask you for $97.00 plus (S&H).

BUT wait. There's more.

In addition to this incredibly low amount, I'm going to "sweeten the pot" by giving you 3 FREE Gifts that will help you even more. Look below and see what I mean:

Free Gift #1 – *Deep Inside the Royal Court DVD* – This DVD will teach you the deep inner-workings of the three most powerful exercises in *Combat Conditioning*. Follow the instructions on this DVD and the magic power of these exercises will totally transform your body from mush to streaming steel.

Free Gift #2 – *How to Eat More and Weigh Less* – This special report reveals the one secret that helps you lose weight without dieting. This one simple change will revolutionize your life and you'll never guess what it is until after you've read the report.

Free Gift #3 – *3 FREE Months of access to the Furey Faithful Membership Site* – (no hidden charges afterward) – this

alone is worth at least $995.00 because you get access to over four years worth of special reports, newsletters and video that members rave about each and every day.

If I were your brother, I'd tell you to drop everything you're doing and order a copy of *The Combat Conditioning System* immediately. It'll change your life more than you can currently imagine.

Claim your copy NOW.

Best,

Matt Furey

Matt Furey

P.S. Have you taken a look at the 3 Free Gifts you receive along with your copy of *The Combat Conditioning System*? These are guaranteed to transform the way you look and feel, faster and easier than you can currently imagine.